STANDING
ON THE
PROMISES

L E W I S   S M E D E S

THOMAS NELSON PUBLISHERS
Nashville

Published in Nashville, Tennessee, by Thomas Nelson, Inc.

Scripture quotations are from the NEW KING JAMES VERSION of the
Bible. Copyright © 1979, 1980, 1982, Thomas Nelson, Inc., Publishers.

Library of Congress Cataloging-in-Publication Data
Smedes, Lewis B.
    Standing on the promises : keeping hope alive for a tomorrow we
cannot control / Lewis Smedes.
        p.   cm.
    Includes bibliographical references.
    ISBN 0-7852-7008-6 (hc)
    1. Hope—Religious aspects—Christianity. I. Title.
BV4638.S56   1998
234'.25—dc21   98–26724
                                                                 CIP

Printed in the United States of America
1 2 3 4 5 6 7 BVG 04 03 02 01 00 99 98

To

Harry Boer,

Jan and Alan Pauw, and

Joan and George Stob

I count myself in nothing else so happy

As in a soul remembering my good friends.

—William Shakespeare

CONTENTS

ACKNOWLEDGMENTS

I want to express my gratitude to several friends for what they have done to help me get this book written and published.

Several friends read early drafts and pointed me to the places that needed more work: Maryland poet Roderick Jellema jostled me into a deeper sense of awe and wonder at the miracle of hope; Esther and Max DePree pooled their insights and made suggestions that contributed richly to later drafts; Dr. Mary Rotzien, whose vision of hope for abused children in Los Angeles is celebrated in the book, helped me toward a truer insight into some of the people whose hopes and dreams I talk about in the book; and Rita Holmes of the Sandra Dijkstra Agency contributed an intuitive literary intelligence that never once failed to help me and sometimes rescued me. Then there are my good friends of the *"Kinder and Gentler Superannuated Critics Club"* I mention them by name to hold them indirectly accountable for the final product whose first draft they so kindly and gently assaulted: Alice and Arthur Glasser, Mary and Robert Meye, Margaret and Robert Shaper, Suzanne and Newton Maloney.

Sandra Dijkstra, the best of all possible agents, danced me through the thickets of the publishing world into my new and happy association with Thomas Nelson Publishers, Inc.

Which brings me to Rolf Zettersten, the publisher, whose commitment to and trust in the book has been genuine and inspiriting; to Curtis Lundgren, editorial director, whose judgment has been flawless, whose enthusiasm has been contagious, and whose discernment has opened my own eyes time and again to ways of improving the manuscript; and to Cindy Blades, managing editor, who has been ever so accommodating to my idiosyncrasies and so generous with her time, her full attention, and her personal care for the project.

I thank Betsy and Sam Reeves who invited Doris and me to use their lovely seaside home as an undisturbed retreat for final revisions.

Doris, my wife of fifty years who knows my dark self-doubts and my pitiful hunger for encouragement and also knows a bad sentence when she reads one, never let her love for me dampen her aspirations for a bit more elegance; I consider her to be my co-author.

Finally, I thank the Lord for giving me the desire, the dream, and the faith to keep my hope for the book alive until the day of its appearance.

FOREWORD

THE SEED FOR THIS BOOK was sown in my mind on a grizzly morning in May of 1992 among ashes still warm after the flaming human horror commonly known as the Los Angeles riots. A friend whose home is near the center of the firestorm led my wife, Doris, and me from charred ruin to charred ruin, from burned-out hope to burned-out hope, each sad scene seducing us closer to the gully of despair. Nothing that I had ever experienced in my life left me feeling more hopeless than the foul stench of despair that hung over the smoldering hulks left over from that one mad night.

A few weeks later, driving away late at night from the Los Angeles County Airport, my mind fixed only on the magic moment when my garage door would curl open and let me snuggle back into my comfortable cocoon, I was jolted to attention by a brilliant billboard towering above Airport Boulevard with just three words in huge, arresting red: KEEP HOPE ALIVE.

In the years since I experienced this mesmerizing epiphany, it has grown in height and breadth until now it seems to fill all the open sky above the city. Now I wonder sometimes whether the billboard I saw was only inside of my own mind, maybe a summons from God or from my own soul to devote whatever remains of my life to keeping hope alive.

Whether literal reality or inner vision, that bright billboard was my awakening to the fact that there is nothing more important in this whole world than keeping hope alive in the human spirit. I am convinced that hope is so close to the core of all that makes us human that when we lose hope we lose something of our very selves. And in the process we lose all reason for striving for the better life we were meant to live, the better world that was meant to be. Let me put it as baldly as I can: there is nothing, repeat nothing, more critical for any one of us, young or old or anywhere in between, than the vitality of our hope.

My arousal to the supreme importance of hope has led my thoughts step-by-step into its mystery, its catalytic power, its risks, the certain death to our spirits when we lose it, and its energy to keep us walking into God's future when we fear what it may bring.

What *is* this thing called hope? What goes on inside of us when we hope? Why do we need hope for our spirits the way we need air and water for our bodies? Why is hope as crucial to our lives as our sanity? Why do some people always abound in hope and others always slouch to despair? How can we become more hopeful persons? How can we keep on hoping when our fondest hopes crash on the rugged edges of tragedy?

Hope is a gift waiting for all who have—*a powerful wish for life to be better than it is, the imagination to look beyond the bad that is to the good that can be, the faith to believe that the good they imagine and wish for is possible.*

Hope is the thing with feathers -
That perches in the soul -
And sings the tune without the words -
And never stops - at all.

And sweetest - in the Gale - is heard -
And sore must be the storm -
That could abash the little Bird
That kept so many warm -

I've heard it in the chillest land -
And on the strangest Sea -
Yet, never, in extremity,
It asked a crumb - of Me.
                                   —Emily Dickinson

Part One
The Basics: What Everyone Needs
to Know About Hope

Chapter 1

❧

BRED IN THE BONE

While Abraham was trekking across the desert in the hope of finding the land that God had promised him, and, four hundred years later, while Moses was leading Abraham's children out of Egypt's bondage in the hope of getting back to the promised land, and, even later, while angels sang the good news that Jesus was newly born in Bethlehem to bring a new hope to all people,

doting grandparents, in a land where no one had heard of Abraham or of Moses or of Jesus, were nestling their grandchildren in their laps and telling them stories of how the gods brought hope to the earth.

They had never heard the Bible's stories of hope, but these ancient storytellers knew in their hearts that all men and all women must live by hope. And so each generation in turn told stories to keep hope alive in the hearts of the children. The story of Pandora and her box was probably the one they told most often. It went something like this.

One day the great god Zeus came down from Mt. Olympus to have a look at the earth. What he found was a global glob of shapeless sludge. No dry land, no pure water, no air, no light, no life—only black, lifeless muck. He did not like what he saw. So he drained the earth, separated the water, poured it into oceans and lakes, and then blew his breath hard enough to spread air over all the earth.

But there were no animals and not a single human being anywhere. Zeus instructed two lesser gods to create some animals and make a man to live on the earth. They did that, and made a fine man, too, but the earth was too dark for him to see and too cold for him to bear. So one of the gods flew up to heaven, stole a flame from the sun, came back to earth, and gave it to man. Now man had light for his mind and warmth for his body. But he lacked one thing.

He did not have a woman.

Seeing how badly the man needed a woman, Zeus ordered his finest artists to make one for him. High on Mt. Olympus, the artists created the most lovely being imaginable and gave her, besides her great beauty, all the graces of wisdom and art. They named her Pandora, which means "someone with all the gifts."

Zeus gave Pandora a treasure chest crammed with everything a man and woman would need to live happily forever. The chest was sealed, and Zeus sternly warned Pandora that only the gods were allowed to open it. Then he sent her down to earth with her chest to be a blessing to man.

But when she got to earth, her curiosity got the better of her, and she pried open the lid to steal a look. All the blessings flew out of the chest and scattered themselves above the earth just out of man's reach. He could see them, and he had a great desire for them, but he could not get them in his grasp.

One blessing stayed in the chest, however, for both man and woman to keep. It was the blessing of hope. And as long as man and woman kept hope alive, they would have the will and the strength to keep on stretching and striving and waiting for the blessings that had flown beyond their reach.[1]

The ancient story of Pandora and her hope chest reveals to us that hope is native to all creation and that all people have always known in their hearts that they could not live without hope.

Hope is bred in the bone. Our spirits were made for hope the way our hearts were made to love and our brains were made to think and our hands were made to make things. Our hearts are drawn to hope as an eagle is drawn to the sky. A "life instinct" is what Karl Menninger called hope.[2] Keep hoping, you keep living. Stop hoping, you die. Inside.

I do not hope because I am a Christian[3] any more than a Jew hopes because she is a Jew. I hope because I am an anxious, struggling, suffering, longing, unfulfilled creature on the way to a future over which I have no control. My faith gives me God as my special reason to keep hoping when fear gets a grip on my soul. And it gives me, I believe, God's own vision of good things that He promises and that I hope for. But, one way or the other, all people hunger for hope because our Maker made us all to live by hope.

What is there about the way He made us that gives us such a need for hope?

First, God gave us the power to imagine the future but gave us no power to control it.[4] We can imagine good things that we *want* to happen, but we cannot *see to it* that they *will* happen. We can also imagine bad things that we do not want to happen, but we cannot *see to it* that they *won't* happen. We can only hope for the good things we imagine while we fear the bad things we imagine.

Second, God made us to be travelers, people on the way.[5] Pilgrims we are, the lot of us, trying to make some progress, on the move, not so much from place to place as from time to time. There is no getting out of it; we must keep moving from now to later, and since we cannot be sure of what comes later, we hope that what comes tomorrow will be better than what came yesterday.

To make these big concepts a little more concrete, I recall the simplest of all parables.

To live the human life is something like taking a long hike on a crooked trail up a rocky hill to a place at the crest where we will have all that our soul longs for. Things like lasting love, good health, peace of mind, joy of heart, and, to make life completely blessed, a close friendship with God. The hill is not all that steep, amateur climbers in reasonably good shape can manage it, but there are obstacles at every twist of the trail: rapid streams without bridges; logs fallen over the path; the trail is fiendishly slick. And there are temptations to give up the journey and settle where we are: wondrous vistas, campsites so comfortable we hate to leave them, and contented folk we meet along the way who tell us that things there are as good as they can get. But we keep climbing.

What keeps us going? Only one thing provides strength for the journey: it is the hope that we will make it to the top. Or at least closer than we've come so far.

This is the serendipity of creation: God has given us the gift of hope to keep us going on our uncertain journey.

But hope can get sick and die. Sometimes hope is murdered with shocking quickness when the one thing on which we set our deepest hope is blown out of our lives, like a tent in the path of a hurricane. Other times hope dies slowly, sliced away in bits and pieces of disappointment, one thing after another that we had hoped for whittled away, like wood chips flying from a green branch before the knife of an indifferent whittler. Whether it slips slowly like drippings from a leaking valve or gets smashed on the rocks of reality, when hope dies inside of us, we are all but done for.[6] *There is nothing more important to the success of our journey to a future we cannot control than that we keep our hope alive.*

ↂ

Just Remember This . . .

> *Bred in the bone, generic human hoping, the hope we are born for, is what we have been talking about. Hope is the Creator's implant into us, His traveling children, on the move into a future we can imagine but cannot control. Hope is our fuel for the journey. As long as we keep hope alive, we keep moving. To stop moving is to die of hope deficiency.*

Chapter 2

❧

THE STUFF HOPE IS MADE OF: WISHING

We do not decide to hope the way we decide to clean the garage on a Saturday morning instead of playing golf. Nobody takes a day off from the office to catch up on his hoping. Hope comes alive on its own when three ordinary inner experiences converge inside of us. To keep hope alive, we need all three. One is two too few. Two is one too few. Hope needs the three of them together, the way fire needs heat and fuel and oxygen—all three—to keep the flame alive.

Here, then, are the three ingredients that keep every hope alive: wishing, imagining, and believing.

We begin with *wishing*.

The whisper of a wish, like the cry of a newborn child, is the first sure sign that hope is being born—an early yearning, a late longing, sometimes a passion, but at least a desire. We only hope for what we wish for. Wish not, hope not.

Somewhere the poet T. S. Eliot quipped that the Maker of

the universe exults in every newly fanned desire. God wants us to wish, I think, because when we have no more wishes to wish, our hope dies of premature contentment. And when I think about the best things in life that I have long wished for, I am encouraged by C. S. Lewis' remark that "Our best havings are our wantings."[1]

Every wish is conceived under the sheets of discontent. We wish for what we do not have and without which we cannot be satisfied with what we do have.

The Bible teaches us to be content in whatever state we find ourselves, a fact that makes some people leery of wishing for too much. Do not wish for much, my mother told me, for wishing is a sign of discontent with what God has given. And, besides, if you wish for too much you will grieve the more when your wishes die unfulfilled. Mother was right in her way. Discontent *is* a snare. When we scratch the itching of our discontent the scratching only makes it worse.

"Question your desires," warned Shakespeare. "Thou shalt not covet," commands the Torah. Why these warnings? Surely not because there is something sinister about wishing. Is it not because we are all tempted to wish for things that, should we get them, can make us wish we had never wished for them?

Yet, how can we be content with our world the way it is? How can we be content with ourselves the way we are? The satisfied soul is a soul that has settled too soon for what *is*. The soul alive with hope is a soul that feels a white-watered undercurrent of wishes for better things. We must be discontent until we find our contentment, eventually, in the fuller, better life that only God can give.

Until then, the trick is to live content with our discontentment.

To achieve contentment with our discontent is to achieve the only kind of peace available to a hopeful spirit. Contentment with discontent is what we call patience. And patience is the spirit's silent strength to wait until it has what it hopes for.

Stop and think for a moment about this deep paradox of the hopeful life: to be content in whatever state we are[2] is the wisdom to accept with gratitude the experience of *not* having what we wish for. Mark this well. We *cannot* be content with the way things are as long as things are not the way we wish them to be. Or the way they ought to be. But we *can* be content to live with our discontent until they get to be the way we hope they will be. Contented discontent is hope's patient impatience.

I will risk a personal example. I was a teacher for a whisker short of forty years, and I was never, not ever, not for a single day in any of those forty years, the teacher I wished to be. Nor the teacher I believed I could be. At the end of every school year, I felt the sort of discontent with myself that a baseball player who is used to winning must feel after a middling season. But every fall when school began again, I felt a new surge of hope that this might be the year when I actually did my job the way I felt it should be done. This Indian-summer hope kept me content to live with my discontent, and it was hope that made my discontented life of teaching a life for which to be very grateful.

For want of a wish, we have no yearning. For want of a yearning, we have no hope. For want of a hope, we have no life.

◦⚬◦

Just Remember This . . .

Wishing for something is the first blush of hoping for it. We do not hope simply because we are told there is something that we should hope for. We never really hope for anything unless we wish it first. If you wonder whether you really do hope for something, ask yourself this: How much do I wish for it?

Chapter 3

❦

THE STUFF HOPE IS MADE OF:
IMAGINING

To see *beyond* what is to what can be. Or to see *within* what seems to be to what *really* is. This is imagination. There can be no hope without it.

We may see it fantastically, as dreamers in restless nights see sublime and hideous things beyond the horizon of sense. We may see it through a gauze dimly or a glass darkly, as an old man sees the world through cataracts. But if we see it at all, and if we wish for what we see, we are on the verge of hoping for it.

The link between imagination and hope is broken if we think that imagination is *only* for such things as fables, fantasies, and fairy tales. We do imagine things that are not real, thank God; what should we do without fairy stories and happy endings? But imagining things is also a way of seeing the most real things of all, things for which we need lenses in our souls as well as in our heads.

Any of us with a wee bit of imagination can see some

realities beyond what floats in front of our noses. And we can see some unnoticed seed of better reality tucked inside the shell of a bad reality. The power to see reality *beyond* the reality we see and touch, we can call *outsight*. The power to see potential reality *inside* of what already is, we can call *insight*.

With *outsight* we see beyond the way things are to the way things ought to be: beyond present misery to future joy, beyond present pain to future healing, beyond present evil to future good, beyond present problems to future possibilities.

With *insight* we see the potential in the present broken world for being the better world it can be. We see the potential in our laggard children for the achieving adults they can be. With insight, we see the pain behind the smile, the decency behind the gruffness, the strength within the humility, the ugliness within the dazzle—and the dormant conscience behind the stone face of indifference.

When I recall my mistakes as a parent of three children, I repent for the times I was so blinded by the goofing off I saw on the surface that I lost my insight into the potential at the depths. And I repent even more so for the times when I discouraged them from imagining fantastic things for themselves. Why did I discourage my son from imagining himself as the first baseman for the Los Angeles Dodgers? Why did I discourage my daughter from imagining herself as the lead singer with Fleetwood Mac?

I can tell you why. It was the same sorry reason my mother warned me against my "big ideas" (her term for bright dreams): I did not want them to be disappointed. Yes, I had good intentions. But I also know that to puncture a child's dream even before she gets a chance to believe in it is a sin.

Martin Luther King's power to keep hope alive in his

people depended utterly on his ability to keep them focused beyond the abuse and degradation they saw with their eyes to a land where life could be decent and fair to all. Whenever he blurred the vision, he weakened the hope. On August 28, 1963, Dr. King gathered 250,000 people at the Lincoln Memorial in Washington, D.C., to make a massive appeal to the conscience of America. But the president's worried men feared trouble if this huge crowd of people got too excited, and they persuaded Dr. King to keep his rhetoric cool. Dr. King gave in to them; he read a careful, thoughtful speech that seemed deliberately devised to keep all hearts from flaming.

The beloved singer Mahalia Jackson, sitting behind him on the platform, felt let down by the speech. When King finished talking and was turning to sit down, she shouted out to him: "The dream, Martin, the dream! Tell them about the dream, Martin! Tell them about the dream!"[1]

King turned back to face the throng and told once more, for the hundredth time, his dream of an America yet to be.

> I have a dream that one day on the red hills of Georgia the sons of former slaves and the sons of former slave owners will be able to sit down together at the table of brotherhood.

> I have a dream that my four little children will one day live in a nation where they will not be judged by the color of their skin but by the content of their character.

King saw beyond the injustice in the America that *was* to the more just America that *could be*. This was his outsight. He also saw, beneath the crust of America's indifference, a dormant conscience waiting to be awakened. This was his insight.

And when he inspired other people to see what he saw, he brought African-Americans to the very threshold of hope.

Who could not imagine a picnic on a red hill in Georgia where children of black slaves and white slave owners were sharing each other's bread? It is the same with the imagination of the Bible. Who could not imagine a world where lions lie down with lambs, where nobody gets sick and dies, and where no tears are ever shed?

"There is in the imagination a sense," says philosopher Mary Warnock, "that there is always more to experience and more in experience than we can predict."[2] This is why every unborn embryo can be a child of hope. Why every moment of imperfect love is a sign of hope for love more perfect. Why every belly laugh is a sign of hope for deeper joy. Why every child's stutter is a sign of hope for a child's song. And why every freedom won, every wrong righted, every wound healed, every gift given, and every alienated person reconciled to another are signs of hope for the kingdom of God.

It is clear enough, then, that we hope for only the things we wish for and only the things we imagine having.

Still, wishing and imagining are not enough. One of the more exciting boyhood dreams I dreamed was that I had become the conductor of the Philadelphia Symphony Orchestra. I stood in front of the mirror and saw myself before that magnificent ensemble of artists, waving my bare hands (Leopold Stowkowski style) in oceanic swells and holding them in thrall to my interpretation of Brahm's First Symphony. I had the wish, and I saw the vision.

But I had no hope at all of actually becoming the conductor of the Philadelphia Symphony or, for that matter, even of a ragtag band. Why not? For the simplest of reasons: I never

believed that there was any possibility that I ever could. Hope
needs, besides wishing and imagining, a faith that what we
wish and what we imagine is possible.

❧

Just Remember This . . .

*Hope is at the door whenever we see beyond what is to
what can be. And when we see within what is the potential for what it can be. We do not have to see it all, nor
need we see it in fine detail, but we need to see enough
to convince us that what we imagine is what, in our spirit's
deep places, we truly want.*

Chapter 4

∽

THE STUFF HOPE IS MADE OF: BELIEVING

H ope is born the moment we believe that the good things we wish for and imagine having are possible for us to have. The odds may be against us, but hope does not calculate the odds. All hope needs is a belief that what we hope for is possible.

Hope is so closely linked to faith that the two tend to blend into one. The Bible says that "faith [or trust] is the substance of things hoped for."[1] This is true of faith in God, but it is also true of all other faith. No matter what we put our faith *in*, when faith goes, hope goes with it. In some ways, hope *is* faith— faith with its eyes on possibilities for the future.

When reports from the trenches tell us that the battle is going against us, hope digs in and fights another day—but only as long as we believe the battle can still be won. Our faith may be in the rightness of our cause. It may be in our superior numbers, in God, or in ourselves. Whatever we put our faith in, it is our faith that, in "scandalously carefree grace,"[2] takes up the slack when the evidence turns against us.

This is what makes hope different from optimism. Optimists live by evidence and their optimism dies when the hard data point to defeat. People of hope live by faith, and their hope lives on even after the life support of tangible evidence shuts itself off. People of hope dig into their faith and draw on it when the vital signs of reason grow faint. People of hope *have to be* people of faith.

Theologians tend to exaggerate the difference between hope and optimism. Jacques Ellul, a brilliant French theologian, wrote that hope and optimism are not only different from each other, they are incompatible with each other.[3] John Macquarrie, an Oxford scholar, says that optimism is a "mere counterfeit of hope."[4] I think they stretch the point in order to make a stronger case for faith.

I suggest that the difference between hope and optimism lies mostly with hope's greater staying power. Hope keeps going after optimism gives up. I call as a witness Theodor Herzl, the father of the Zionist hope for a modern Jewish state.

Theodor Herzl was born in 1860, the child of rich Jewish parents in Vienna. He ended up living in Paris as a celebrated pundit, journalist, and playwright. Herzl did not want to think of himself as a Jew, did not live in the ghetto with other Jews, did not believe in the God of the Jews. He chose to be a completely modern and secular European.

Yet, thoroughly secular though he was, Herzl had a passionate hope that rested totally on faith.

At first he was convinced that the only way for Jews to deflect the rising anti-Semitism in Europe was to stop being

Jewish. Europeans, he thought, would accept Jews if they would stop thinking of themselves as a special people, get out of the ghetto and live like everyone else.

But then on January 5, 1895, a single event killed Herzl's optimism. An army captain named Alfred Dreyfus was convicted of being a traitor to France. This Dreyfus had been a very model of Herzl's non-Jewish Jew. He had tried to shed his Jewishness in the French army where, he thought, a man was a man and where bravery was the only thing that distinguished one man from another. He had some success; he became an officer. Then he was (falsely) accused of passing French military secrets to the Germans. He was quickly tried, convicted, and paraded through the streets in shame.

What awakened Herzl from his slumbers was a cry that went up from the crowd at the trial: "Death to the traitor; death to the Jews." That cry was the beginning of Herzl's conversion. Now he knew that Dreyfus was not convicted of treason; he was convicted of being a Jew. And he knew in a flash that Jews could never escape their Jewishness by losing themselves in the crowd.

The Jews *were* a special people, always had been a special people, and could be nothing else but a special people. Europeans would hate the Jews whether they lived as an odd people in a ghetto or as modern individuals submerged into Parisian culture. This much Dreyfus taught him.

But how could the Jews survive as an alien people against the rising tide of hatred? There was only one way: the Jews had to become more than just a separate people; they had to become a separate nation. They had to have a Jewish state.

Herzl became a secular prophet, calling God's people back

home to the land of promise. "We are a people, one people" he wrote. "We have everywhere tried honestly to integrate with the national communities surrounding us [but] . . . we are not permitted to do so." At first he believed that it did not matter *where* the Jewish state existed, as long as it was truly Jewish. But then he realized that the only home for the Jews was the land of their fathers, the land of promise—Palestine.

He had no evidence at all that his dream had the slightest chance of coming true. His own newspaper described it as a "madness born of despair." His Jewish friends feared that he had gone crazy. What drove Herzl, however, was not madness, but faith that his vision was a glimpse into reality yet to be.

So he had a wish as compelling as a mother lion's hunger, a vision as clear as the desert sky, and faith as fervent as a fanatic's passion. The three of them fueled his hope the way gasoline fuels a fire.

Herzl's faith-driven hope led him to sacrifice his wealth, his career, and finally his very life for the land he hoped for. He died in 1904, when he was only forty-four years old, exhausted and penniless. But his hope lit a fire in Jewish hearts that, like Moses' burning bush, would not, could not, be consumed.

On Friday, May 14, 1948, in the city of Tel Aviv, David Ben Gurion, the first president of modern Israel, read the following proclamation: "We hereby declare the establishment of a Jewish state in Palestine, which shall be known as the State of Israel."[5]

Unlike Herzl, I am neither secular nor Zionist; I am a believing Christian. Yet, Herzl's hopes were fed by his faith just as my hopes are fed by mine. He hoped for different things than I do, and I believe different things than he did. But without faith neither of us would have had any hope at all.

I believe that one day life will win over death, that good will win over evil, that love will win over hate, that joy will win over sadness, and that the whole world will work the way its Creator intended it to work. I want it desperately, I can imagine what it would be like, and I believe that with God it is possible. I have no hard evidence that such goodness is *likely* to heal our broken world. But I do have my reasons for believing it *can*. The reasons all compress into one: God. God is; therefore I hope. I hope; therefore I am.

These then—wishing, imagining, and believing—are the stuff that hope is made of. Call them the raw materials of hope if you wish. The point is that hope begins to stir in me when I truly wish for things I do not have. It takes on a life of its own when I imagine what it would be like if my wish were granted. And hope arrives ripe and mature when I believe that the dream I want to come true *can* come true.

Just Remember This . . .

Hope comes alive with the birth of faith and stays alive as long as we keep believing. We hope only for what we believe is possible. No matter what we put our faith in, we will sing the song of hope only to the tune of faith. Hope, we could say, is faith with an eye to the future.

Chapter 5

❧

HOPE IS OUR MOST PRECIOUS ENERGY SOURCE

In a worn-out hotel in the seediest part of town, twelve assorted drunks held themselves together by the thread of hope that one day they would stick the cork back in the bottle and go back to real life. Meanwhile they waited for Hickey. Who was Hickey and why did they wait for him? Hickey was a traveling salesman who showed up every couple of months with a few new stories and a few new laughs in his traveling bag to give them a few hours of respite from their desolate boredom. Hickey finally showed up, but this time he brought no funny stories, no laughs, no respite. He had been converted, he said, and had become a sort of preacher.

Hickey didn't preach your standard gospel of salvation from despair. He came to save people from their hopes. Hope is one of those drugs that "ruin a guy's life and keep him from finding any peace." Pipe dreams, Hickey called them. "I know from experience what a lying pipe dream can do to you—and how relieved and contented with yourself you feel when you're rid of it. . . . Let yourself sink down to the bottom of the sea. Rest in peace. . . . Not a single hope or dream left to nag you."

That was Hickey's gospel. Their only hope of salvation was to face up to their own rotten futility and stop hoping. Well, they did face up to it. They gave up hope. And they died. Inside. They all died. Even the booze lost its kick.[1]

Without some hope of getting it done, nobody among all the families of earth through all epochs of time has ever roused his will and set his mind to do something that needed doing.

Has any mason ever put brick to mortar who did not have hope of finishing a wall? Has any writer ever put a word to paper without hoping that more and better words would follow? Has any entrepreneur ever begun a project without hope of pushing it into production and success? Has any painter ever put a brush to canvas who did not hope that he would create a small world of beauty on it? Has any addicted person ever broken his addiction without hope that he could do it? And have any two persons healed their wounded marriage without hope that the marriage was healable?

One early evening as the dusk darkened the always shadowed Sistine Chapel, Michelangelo, weary, sore, and doubtful, climbed down the ladder from his scaffolding where he had been lying on his back since dawn painting the chapel ceiling. After he had eaten a lonely supper, he wrote a sonnet to his aching body. The last line of his sonnet astonished me when I first came upon it at an exhibition of the master's sketches and the memory of it has comforted me in my times of self-doubt: "I am no painter."

But when the sun shone again, Michelangelo got up from his bed, climbed back up on his scaffold, and labored another day on his magnificent vision of the Creator at work on His brand-new world. What pushed him up the ladder? Could it have been anything but a hope born again from a night's rest, a hope just strong enough to keep the doubts in check for another day, a hope that became the energy to paint the greatest picture of them all?

Infinitely removed in significance, but not much different in the feeling, is a hunch I have had about this book every time I sat down to write. Why go on with a piece of work when I do not have the gift to do it the way it deserves to be done? A book on hope needs a poet of hope, one who dreams shimmering dreams and sees heroic visions. "O God, if You had to give me the calling, could You not have given me the talent?" But against the grain of my depressing doubts some gutsy hope that I cannot kill pushes me back to my desk and keeps me there until a decent day's work has been done.

What a discontent there is to life when hope will not let us rest satisfied with where we are. And what a privilege that discontent is. Without it we would never do a single thing that needs doing to bring us where we want to be. As I said early on, contentment with discontent is our key to the restless joys of a hopeful life.

Back in the seventies, I learned something about hope from teaching a seminar on the relationship between faith and political change. I learned that slaves do not break their chains because they are slaves; they break their chains when they find hope that they do not *have* to be slaves anymore. And I learned that hungry people do not change their condition because they are hungry; they change their condition when they find hope that they do not *have* to be hungry.

During the cold war in Czechoslovakia, Vaclav Havel spent half of his days in jail and half of them at a menial job in a state brewery. All the while, however, he was the poet of hope for the Czech people. Finally, the wall came down. Czechoslovakia became a free republic, and Havel became its first president. He was asked to explain how he kept going during those decades of despair. "I am not an optimist," he said, " I am a person of hope. . . . I cannot imagine that I would strive for anything if I did not carry hope in me."

Yes, the power to strive. But hope also gives people the power simply to endure. "How come," asks Jewish philosopher Emil Fackenheim, "Jews are still around after thousands of years, most of them in exile," often persecuted, and sometimes all but annihilated? "There is only one answer," he insists, "and that answer is hope."[2]

I am sitting at my desk in Sierra Madre, California, on a Monday morning because back in 1912, in a plain little village called Garijp plopped in the middle of Friesland—a flat, green province of northernmost Holland—a restless blacksmith by the name of Melle Smedes, twenty-one years old, married Rena Benedictus, a ruddy-faced, plumpish farm girl of twenty, and infected her with his yearning for better things than he could ever provide by pounding an anvil in the family smithy.

Melle had lapped up rumors of the good life in the United States of America that were spreading among poor folk everywhere in Europe. The rumors he heard gave dreamy form to his shapeless longings. And he persuaded himself and then persuaded Rena that he could make his dream come true.

So Melle and Rena invested their substance in a passage, steerage, on a Dutch steamer, left the only people and the only place they had ever known or loved, and sailed west on the winds of hope. They did not know exactly where they were going to settle, did not know a word of English, had no promise of a job and next to nothing in survival funds. But their hope had lit a fire in their innards that drove them across the sea to a future they could barely imagine and certainly could not control.

Now we must make a sudden switch to a very different role that hope plays in our lives. It is the connection between hope and the neurological miracle we call the brain. The brain itself still mystifies us. What triggers the brain to push a brilliant human being into Alzheimer's darkness? How does a drug like Clozapine get the brain to cut the chains that bind the mind of the schizophrenic? And why does it not do its magic for everyone?

We are also mystified by the link between the human brain and the human hope. But that there is a link seems undeniable. Every minute of our lives, the brain is making millions of transactions. Messages zip across electrical pathways and make their marks at the right place in the brain. Some of the messengers are bits of chemicals that talk to brain cells. Some are electronic. But in between it seems likely that spiritual messages of hope for healing get sent to the brain, and the brain sends healing orders back to the body.

The messages of hope somehow link up with the million billion synapses through which the brain sends billions of messages to specific nerve centers that control the organs of the body. The nerve centers then send an E-mail back to the brain: "Orders received, action initiated, healing begun." This is somewhat the way it struck the late Norman Cousins who, after watching patients deal with terminal illness at the UCLA Medical Center for ten years, was convinced that it makes scientific sense to speak of the "biology of hope."[3]

All that I have said in this chapter leads to one conclusion:

Hope is the spiritual power for living successfully as creatures endowed with the Godlike ability to imagine the future but stuck with the humanlike inability to control it. I cannot vouch for the report that he said it, but if he did say it, Martin Luther was seeing reality with his usual clean-sweep vision: "Everything that is done in the world is done by hope."

⌘

Just Remember This . . .

Hope is the energy to strive for what we hope for. We keep striving as long as we keep hoping. If you lose hope, you lose desire, you lose your dream, you lose your faith, and you lose your inner power to strive for the better future you can imagine but cannot control.

Chapter 6

Hope and Worry Are Sibling Rivals

Worry is hope's bothersome twin brother. Hope keeps us going, and worry makes us careful on the way. Life being what it is, threats to it swirl around us in swarms, stare us hard in the face—stubborn, ever-present, real, tough. So hope is always butting heads with worry.

Worry is forever trying to take the wind out of hope's sails. Hope is forever resetting its sails to whatever wind there is. Sometimes hope gets the better of worry; sometimes worry pins hope to the mat. But we are stuck with both of our fighting siblings.

I learned something about hope and worry in the confusing days that followed hard on the afternoon when doctors told Doris and me that the youngest of our three adopted children, John, four years old at the time, had Gaucher's disease. We had never heard of it. But this much we learned right away: Gaucher's is a genetic foul-up that occurs mostly among Ashkenazi Jews; it happens when the biological apparatus fails to produce the enzymes we need to break down certain lipids (fatty cells) that the body keeps producing. The lipids get into the bloodstream, and there is no safe parking place for them. But park they do. And wherever they settle, they do several sorts of damage, some acute and deadly to little children, others chronic and troublesome to older children and adults.

The prognoses for victims of John's age were cloudy at the time. He was borderline; he was at an age when he could have had either the acute or the chronic form. He could, we were told, live into adolescence, possibly longer, but no promises. Only possibilities.

We wrung some symbolic significance out of the name of the hospital: The City of Hope. And we did hope. We put our hope in God. We put our hope in medical research. And our hope was fulfilled; it turned out that he had the chronic form of the disease. But our hope was never for a moment without worry.

Sometimes, when people cannot cope with the tension between worry and hope, they get relief from worry by giving up hope.

A study was once made of how American airmen coped with their fear of dying during World War II. Many of them conquered fear by giving up on hope. Many airmen just "stopped giving a hoot." They stopped believing that survival was possible; the odds against it were too bad. They stopped fantasizing about what life would be like when the war was over. So they also stopped wishing for V-day. Thus, hope wilted into indifference. Whatever will be will be, they figured, so chugalug, and stop hoping.

But when they had only a few missions left before going

on a furlough, their whole attitude changed. They started to give a hoot again. They wished for it like a dog wishing to get off a leash, they imagined themselves lounging at a resort, and they again believed that survival for that day was possible. In short, when relief was in sight, they hoped again. But at a price. For the moment they began to hope, they also began to worry.[1]

Another way we escape the tension is by becoming fatalistic about our lives. Some people convince themselves that only bad things can happen to them. Others con themselves into believing that only good things can happen to them. Either way, the dice are loaded. The script is written. The fight is fixed. We are de-hoped. There is no point in worrying if fate seals your failure *or* your success. So why worry? And why hope?

Some people try to use faith as a wedge into the worry-free life. But faith does not put worry to sleep. Hope is the child of faith, and worry is the child of doubt. But doubt is the twin sister of faith. The French theologian Ellul had it just right: "The person who is plunged into doubt is not the unbeliever but the person who has no other hope but hope."[2] Unbelievers do not have to doubt. Believers *doubt* precisely because they live by faith and not by sight. And they *hope* precisely because they live by faith. So worry tags along with doubt as long as we live by faith and hope.

One of the more hopeful ways of expressing faith is to say that, while we do not know what the future holds, we know who holds the future. But not even this assurance keeps us from worrying, for the future that God holds still brims with both threats and possibilities. God deals the cards, but we don't know which cards He may deal us tomorrow. We hope He will deal us a strong hand, while we worry that He will deal us a weak hand.

So as long as we have something to hope for we will have something to worry about. And as long as we worry about it, we know that the embers of hope are still burning within us.

∽

Just Remember This . . .

> We hope for good things that we cannot be sure of getting. Not being sure, we tend to worry. But we should not worry too much about worry; it comes with being spirits who can imagine the future and cannot control it. The trick is to develop a strong enough faith to keep worry in its place and then use worry to make us wise and careful in our hoping. If we ever come to the point where we never worry, we have reached either the happy point where we do not need to hope or the bitter point where we cannot hope.

Chapter 7

∽

HOPE IS STRENGTH TO DO NOTHING BUT WAIT

I arrived at a hotel in Minneapolis at two-thirty on a dog-day afternoon, dripping sweat, tired from travel, and straining to get into an air-conditioned room where I could take a shower, rest, and look at my notes for a lecture I was scheduled to give at four o'clock. My hopes were challenged by the clerk at the desk.

"We cannot give you a room yet, sir. The computers are down."

"How long will it take to fix them?"

"We can't say for sure. I suggest you wait in the lounge."

I took a chair where I could keep my eyes on the clerk. I chafed, I fretted, I growled. I got up and shuffled over to the desk every five minutes and grumbled my way back to my chair. And waited some more.

Two middle-aged couples sitting at a table next to me sipped their chardonnay, roaming the lobby with lazy eyes that saw nothing, not even each other. Now and then one of the males would mutter something inane about women who walked by, and the other would mutter, "Yeah."

Twiddling our thumbs until whatever is going to happen happens—this is not waiting. It is what psychologist Erich Fromm called a "disguised form of hopelessness."[1]

We *choose* to wait when we want what we wait for. We *have* to wait for it because we can do nothing to make it happen. We *are able* to keep waiting for it only as long as we keep believing it will happen. Waiting is in the wanting, in the helplessness, and in the believing. But it is the helplessness that makes waiting so cold, so lonely, and sometimes so paralyzing.

I knew a man who had much power over many people. But he waited in helpless terror for his eighteen-year-old son who was wandering alone, an aimless minstrel in a far country, never writing, never calling.

"What can I do?" asked the man who every day told others to go and they went and told them to come and they came.

"There is nothing you can do, but wait and hope and pray, and wait."

"Ah, the waiting, the waiting. It's so hard, I'm not sure I can stand it."

I have now and then had to endure the same helpless waiting that my friend was feeling. There was a time recently when our son, the one with a genetic blood malady—the one we worry too much about—had been incommunicado for a few weeks. He had just come away from a seven-month siege of smashing, brass-knuckled pain. He had decided earlier that his life would be simpler (for him) if he got rid of his telephone. But there was still E-mail and an 800 number at work, so he could have called, as he always has. But this time he didn't return our calls for longer than we were used to.

In my helplessness, I wrung my hands. He knows that I worry a lot; *why* didn't he call? I couldn't sleep. I imagined the worst possible scenarios. I saw calamity and sorrow ahead: maybe he was fired from his job, was kicked out of his apartment, and was wandering alone in the streets. I feared that his time of trouble had come heavy upon him. As hard as any waiting must be, I made it ten times harder than it had to be by my lack of faith. Still, I could not stop waiting for the call.

Finally it came. Calamity and sorrow had not fallen on him. He had reasons for not calling. I vowed never to worry again, knowing that I would.

Nelson Mandela had to wait in prison for twenty-seven years before his hope of a new South Africa could be achieved. As the day of his freedom drew close, his only daughter was allowed to come and see him. When she came she carried with her the grandchild Mandela had never seen. She had waited to name the child until her grandfather could give her a name. "I don't think a man was ever happier to hold a baby than I was that day," he wrote in his memoirs. Mandela named her Zaziwe, an African word for hope. He called her Hope, he said, because "during all my years in prison hope never left me—and now it never would."[2]

What we often forget is that though worry is almost automatic, we have to make a decision, many decisions sometimes, to keep on waiting. People will tell us to give it up, to let hope die and let worry die with it. And they have us almost convinced. But we decide to keep on waiting. And our decision to keep waiting shapes our whole living.[3]

If we could just get rid of the hoping, waiting would come

easier, but then our waiting would be soaked in dirty, gray boredom like a mop in lukewarm scum, and this would not be real waiting at all. "I said to my soul, be still, and wait without hope" goes T. S. Eliot's despairing line. But the soul cannot wait without hope. We stop waiting as soon as we stop hoping. Eliot's later line clears the air: "But the faith and the love *and the hope* are all in the waiting."[4]

In his memorable book, *Man's Search for Meaning*, Viktor Frankl helped us comprehend the waiting power of hope. He told us about Jews who kept waiting for the day they would get out of their concentration camps when any eye could see they would die there. They kept waiting because they kept hoping. But what earthly good did it do them to wait for what was so unlikely to happen?

Frankl's answer was that in waiting for escape those Jews were making a claim on their own sacred identity and the meaning and purpose of their lives. The guards drummed it into their heads every hour that they were pigs, vermin, scum of the earth. But as long as they remembered that they were the children of God, they kept on waiting. And as long as they waited, they maintained the dignity of the children of God.

The people who kept on waiting walked erect. They talked lively talk together, and they argued eye to eye with God. They made music. They kept up their humane civilities with one another to show that they remembered that their doomed lives had more point and purpose than the lives of the guards who would murder them.

I must say one more thing about waiting: we do not wait in hope only because there is nothing we can do. Sometimes we wait in hope only *after* we have done all that we can do.

The growing of grapes and the making of wine are parables

of the waiting that follows the working. The grower plants his vines, prunes them, and nourishes them. But having done all that he can do, he is helpless against the blights, the birds, the frosts, the floods—helpless against the forces of nature that pool their powers to determine the quality of the grape.

The wine *maker* controls the choice and the crushing of the grapes, controls the time the skin stays in the juice, controls the choice of barrels—the more expensive French oak from a forest in the Alsace with its stronger aroma or the more available American oak with its subtler aroma—and she controls the blending of the juices and the time the wine shall be in the barrel. Every stage is in her hands. But when the wine is finally in the barrel, she loses control. Now she, too, can only wait to see what wine will pour from the blend brooding in the cool of the cave.

It is hard, this interminable waiting. Nobody likes to wait when waiting seems forever. So I come back again to the secret of being at peace with ourselves when we have to wait a long time for what we hope for: it is the discovery that we can be content with our discontent. Discontent is the way of the traveling life, and we are all born to travel; we are discontent until we get to where we hope to be, but as long as we have hope of getting there, we can be content with the discontent of not being there yet.

∾

Just Remember This . . .

Waiting is our destiny as creatures who cannot by themselves bring about what they hope for. We wait in the darkness for a flame we cannot light, we wait in fear for a happy ending we cannot write. We wait for a not yet that feels like a not ever.[5] *Waiting is the hardest work of hope.*

Chapter 8

❧

A Time to Stop Hoping?

For two years Delia Menzies and her husband, Pan, have been fighting a losing war against a boiling volcano on their island home of Montserrat in the Caribbean Sea. Two times in these two years the volcano has attacked them and beat them down. The first time its lava and ashes buried their home and their farm. But they built another house and kept hoping the volcano would not erupt and cover them again.

It did. In a tidal wave of boiling mud it came, as a steaming avalanche it came, and it buried their house the second time. Only this time it was infinitely worse—their son was buried alive inside their buried house.

Now the schools are closed. The airport is down. The island is cut off from the mainland world for days at a time. Half of the people have left Montserrat for good. But not Delia and Pan. They are staying on. Why?

Why do people like them stick with sinking ships? There is only one reason, one reason under the bright Caribbean sun: they stay, they say, because they hope that the next time the lava will flow the other way.

Every hopeful fisherman has to cut bait sometime. Is there also a time to stop hoping for our life's deepest desires? A time for families of missing soldiers to stop hoping their sons and lovers will come home alive? A time for a wife to stop hoping that her husband will survive his tumor? A time for a gambler to stop hoping that her long shots will ever pay off? A time for Delia and Pan to give up and leave their sun-burned island?

Does anyone know for sure when the time has come to quit hoping? Deciding that the time has come to stop hoping may be just about the hardest thing we ever do. And God does not give us a stopwatch to tell us when the time has come. We can only watch and pray and listen for the winds of wisdom.

Betty Fredman was having guests at a backyard barbecue on her husband Fred's thirtieth birthday. They forgot to watch the open door for two distracting minutes, which was enough time for their toddler, Kevin, to slip through it and tumble over the edge of the swimming pool.

In the emergency room the medics immediately attached him to a respirator. But an encephalogram showed that the cortex of the brain was virtually dead. Their physician advised the Fredmans that if Kevin stayed on the respirator for a few more days, his heart would get strong enough to beat without help and he might then survive, but only as a vegetable, for twelve or thirteen years. The doctor asked their permission to disconnect the respirator.

But when they pricked Kevin's feet with a pin, he winced and sometimes opened his eyes. Then their minister called to mind that where life is, there hope is, and that where God is, all things can be hoped for. So resting their hope in God, they left Kevin on the respirator for six more days before they took him off. After they removed the respirator, his heart kept pumping blood into his veins, and his lungs kept sending oxygen into his brain stem.

That was five years ago. Kevin has never opened his eyes or moved his arms again and exists today in what is euphemistically called a persistent vegetative state. But is the body that lives and breathes really Kevin?

Daring to stop hoping when we reach hope's limits can sometimes give us the chance to discover a deeper hope to live by. Or die by.

Consider the stories of two close friends. One of them is Sally; the other is Charity. Sally, earlier on, had contracted polio. When she first learned she had it, she wanted to give up. But Charity talked her into hope. So she did hope, and her hope energized her to make a very good life for herself, polio and all.

Then it was Charity's turn. She got cancer. But Charity did not want hope. And she did not want Sally to persuade her to hope as she had persuaded Sally.

But Sally persisted: "It isn't like you, Charity. When I was sick and wanting to die, you sat by my bed . . . and wouldn't let me give up hope."

"Bless you," said Charity. "It was different with you. I wanted you to hope because hope could make you well. You just had to set your will on it. But hope would be foolish for me. It wouldn't do me any good. . . . They just sewed me up again, and I had to learn to face the facts, and make the most of what time I had left."[1]

In the end, death has no respect for hope; hoping hard against that dark night does not make the sun shine a minute longer. At some moment that we cannot postpone, we will get to the finish line; we are going to die. The door of our most vital hope will close and, if we know it is closing, we are wise indeed to quit hoping for it to stay open.

There *is* a time to hope and a time not to hope. It is not wise to hope for things that *cannot* happen. It is not right to hope for things that *should not* happen.

First, a word about not hoping for *impossible* things.

"Man has legs but not wings; he can walk but cannot fly."[2] And if he hopes to fly without wings his hope is maneuvering him into self-delusion. When our desires become delusions and our delusions become our hopes, we are dallying with great grief.[3] The doctrine that everything is possible for everyone is a hoax.

Being born sets a limit to hope like nothing else does. Birth plunks us, without our advice or consent, into the circumscribed setting where we are born. We begin our small life stories wherever we were dropped off. And we have to write them with the raw materials set aside for us before we arrived.

Each of us is handed his or her own stock of genetic raw materials; some of us inherit a genetic fortune, others of us begin with a genetic deficit. Again at birth, and again without being consulted, we were delivered into the hands of parents who may be a blessing to us or they may be a bane.

The distribution of the raw materials for writing our life stories is unfairness itself. So what can we do about it? Nothing? Can we be sure? Who in our dizzying high-tech era dares to say "nothing"?

In 1997 a team of patient Scots produced Dolly, a healthy, newborn sheep conceived, not in animal passion, but from a single cell surgically sliced from an udder belonging to its gentle "mother." As 1998 was hardly under way, a scientist in Chicago told the world that he is already in the process of cloning a human being. In the near future, in fact, we should be able to clone a new human being from cells taken from two aborted fetuses, thus bringing a person into the world whose father and mother were never born.

If you are excited by the possibility of creating a *single carbon copy* of yourself, consider the possibility of determining the lives of *all* of your heirs unto the third and four hundredth generations. Genetic engineers tell us that in twenty years it will be possible to arrange that no heir of ours will ever inherit a disease that has been in our family for years, and for that matter, never even catch a cold. They also tell us that we may be able to decide that all future generations of our offspring will be thin, beautiful, talented, born leaders with intelligence enough to solve most of the world's problems.

It can be done by altering or replacing our faulty genes, those little flecks that draw the blueprints for the way our bodies and minds work. By *altering* the genes in our sperm and eggs, geneticists can *relieve* all future generations from whatever hereditary diseases have plagued our families. By *replacing* the genes, they will be able to *enhance* the lives of all future generations far beyond what they would have been had we left the genes alone. If you pooh-pooh the possibility that it could really happen, just remember Dolly.

But even if it is possible, is it permissible? Should we even desire the power to control the genetic future of our children and our children's children? It must be right for me to hope that genetic engineers can prevent any of my son's offspring from being victims of his disease. But is it right for any of us to hope for the power to endow all our heirs for time to come with the gifts of body and spirit that *we* decide they should have?

Has genetic engineering seduced us beyond the limits of legitimate hope? I for one will need insight that I do not yet have before I can get it into my heart to hope that mere human beings, the best of them sinful and shortsighted, will take over God's prerogative of deciding what life shall be like for all future children until the end of time.

We have been dealing here with two limits to hope: the limit of what is possible and the limit of what is permissible. There is no simple test that will tell us when we have reached the limits and no stopwatch for when to stop hoping. Our only recourse is our discernment and God's guidance.

∞

Just Remember This . . .

> Hope has its limits. Not everything we have it in our hearts to hope for is actually possible. Not everything we get it into our heads to hope for should be hoped for. There are times when it is right to stop hoping for what we know is not possible. There are times when it is wrong to start hoping for what we doubt is right. We are not always sure when we have come to such times. We can be sure, however, that if ever there is a time not to hope for something, there is never a time not to hope at all.

Chapter 9

⊱≾⊰

FALSE HOPE CAN BE WORSE THAN NO HOPE AT ALL

T here are two things that kill the soul, despair and false hope." St. Augustine had a sound intuition when he said that. What makes despair and false hope doubly dangerous is that they have a fatal attraction for each other. When we are sunk in what John Bunyan called "the slough of despair," we are desperate suckers for false hope. And false hope, when we grab for it, is a trapdoor into even deeper despair.

What makes false hope so seductive is that people who have it don't know they have it until it has done its dirty work on them. It wears ten thousand masks and lives ten thousand lives. And the line that divides false from valid hope is often as thin as a filament and wavy as an encephalogram. A desperate person has no eye for fine lines.

So I am going to hazard a short tour through the thickets of false hopes and put some labels on the different species.

The most common false hope is the one aroused by lying promises. A charming salesman persuaded a newly made widow that investments in limited partnerships offered her the best hope of turning her late husband's meager pension into a significant estate. And he just happened to have a perfect deal for her. "Can't possibly fail. Sure to double the principal in three years." Banking on his promises, she sank the whole modest lump into the charmer's enterprise. Three years later, the partnership folded and she did not get back a penny.

When its people are crawling on the border of despair a whole nation can choose to let a ranting messiah mesmerize them with his lying promises. Desperate for any hope of getting out of their miry pit, they hitch their destiny to the hope that their Hitler or their Mao may stir up in them. Their hopes blind them to titanic evils done against their neighbors as well as to the ultimate catastrophe that waits for themselves. The fires of Auschwitz were lit by false hope.

We falsify hope by using hope as an escape from responsibility. Fools make a mess of their lives and then pin their hopes on a kind fate or an indulgent God to rescue them from their folly.

Godfrey Cass was this sort. He had gotten himself deep into a debt so large that he could not pay even the first installment. But he had a big belief in the magic of hope. So he fled to his usual refuge, the hope that a single throw of fortune's dice would save him.

Godfrey was a flawed character in George Eliot's classic novel *Silas Marner*. Here is how George Eliot sized up Godfrey's hope. "Let him live outside his income, or shirk the honest work that brings wages, and he will presently find himself [hoping for] a possible benefactor. . . . Let him betray his friend's confidence and he will adore that . . . cunning complexity called Chance, which gives him the hope that his friend will never know. . . . Let him forsake a decent craft . . . and his religion will infallibly be the worship of blessed Chance, which he will believe in as the mighty creator of success."

I know people who put their hopes in God the way Godfrey Cass put his in Chance. They flounder into a sinkhole of avoidable trouble and sweetly set their hopes on an odd-job god who they expect will drop whatever he is doing and rush to their rescue. Piety and folly are too often wed, and when they are married folly and false hope become one flesh.

We falsify hope by pinning our hope on things that cannot give us what we hope for. Linked to every hope we have for this thing or that thing is a deeper hope for happiness. So when we hope for things to bring us a happiness they cannot possibly give, we are falsifying our hope.

A woman hopes that another face-lift will make her young and desirable again—all she needs to make her happy. A father hopes that his sons will make it big in sales, as he never did, so that he can be happy in their successes as he might have been in his own. A manager of a small firm hopes that by working eighteen hours a day he can satisfy his soul and secure his fortune at the same time. False hopes, all of them, not because they cannot come true, but because even if they do come true they cannot bring the happiness we had hoped they would give us.

A hope that bad things will happen to other people is hope falsified by its own meanness. A scholar secretly hopes that her colleague's new book will get worse reviews than her own book did. A law school graduate hopes that a classmate who has always gotten better grades will not get the good job he hopes for. A failing entrepreneur hopes that his competitor will have a slight heart attack. A mother whose own daughter could not get into college hopes that her friend's daughter will drop out of Vassar and marry a deadbeat.

Any hope for another person's ill is false from the start. And for a simple reason: hope by definition is for good things to happen. Hope for other's ill is a wish for bad things to happen. Hope is one thing; spite is something else.

We falsify hope by hoping that our pain will go away before we give ourselves a chance to feel it. I know a woman who had been deeply hurt by her husband's several affairs with other women. Yet she kept assuring herself that the affairs had not wounded her and that with a bit of help from a therapist, the marriage would quickly be healed. So the two of them hopefully trudged together to a wise counselor, whose opening question for her was:

"Do you have any hope for your marriage after what he has done?"

"Yes, of course I have, I wouldn't be here if I didn't have hope," the woman responded.

"Bad idea. Not time to hope yet," the counselor advised.

"Not time to hope? Why not?"

"You haven't felt the pain yet. You mustn't hope to heal your marriage until you feel the pain of the brokenness and the lie that broke it."

It was a wag with little style but sound insight who said: "Hope is not dope." Nor is it an anesthetic. A hope for healing before we feel the pain is not a hope that we can overcome our pain, but a hope that we will not have to feel it. No honesty in it, it is a false hope.

There is no easy way to tell false hope from honest hope. All we can do is keep our eyes open and our hearts pure so that we can recognize a phony hope when it shows up in front of our noses, seducing us to invest more of our happiness in it than our short lives can afford.

∽∞∽

Just Remember This . . .

> Hope, like love, can be fake. And when it is, we pay heavily for counting on it. A hope may be false because it is based on other people's lies. But it can also be false because we falsify it ourselves. We can use hope as a cheap escape from the messes we create. We turn hope false by expecting a happiness that the thing we hope for cannot bring. We turn hope false when we hope out of a mean spirit. And we turn hope false when we hope to overcome pain before we even feel it.

Chapter 10

༄

CAUTION: HOPE CAN BREAK
YOUR HEART

There is a tense scene in the movie *Schindler's List* when Schindler—the flawed man of business whose daring schemes saved so many Jewish people from death—stood alongside a Nazi officer on the blistering platform of a village station and watched a snake of cattle cars jammed with Jewish people puff in for a quick stop before unloading its doomed human cargo.

The Jews were suffocating. They poked their hands out of cracks between the slats and croaked for water. Schindler saw a couple of fire hoses curled on the platform floor, grabbed one of them, turned on the faucet, and sprayed it through the top cracks, trickling the cold water over the heads of the parched prisoners.

The officer stopped him: "You should not do that. You will give them hope, and that would be cruel."[1]

All hope should come with a sign: CAUTION: HOPE CAN BREAK YOUR HEART. As the renowned psychologist Erich

Fromm wrote: "Hope often is shattered so thoroughly that a man may never recover from it."[2] Hope *can* be cruel.

It took a decade for Rena Benedictus Smedes to learn how cruel hope can be. She lived mostly on the hope she borrowed from my father. She followed his dream to a country spot in Western Michigan named Reeman, a village even smaller and less hopeful than the village they had left behind in Friesland. She bore him four children there and waited for him to make his dreams come true. Nobody could say that he did not try; for nine years he groped from one fallen hope to another.

It was not as if he did not work like a plug horse on his field of dreams. But he did not always have talent to match his dreams; he tried farming when his smithy failed, but his only skill was in smithing. He puttered with gadgets, inventions even, like a gadget for using carbide to light up farms. But his timing was off. Electric lights were already on the way.

Negative reality always seemed to get a jump on his positive dreams. Finally, he put his hopes on a shelf and took the family to Muskegon, Michigan, a working man's foundry town on the east coast of the big lake, and took a seven-to-five immigrant's job, smithing the molds. Only for the time being, of course.

Until he could get his dream back on its feet again. He put in nine-hour shifts at the foundry, and then, each evening until darkness fell, he worked at building his family a house of sorts on Amity Street. He had never built a wall before, and the cement block walls he put up for the basement in the evening collapsed before morning. But he finally did get four walls together and a roof overhead, and the six of them moved in. (I came along a year later.) For my mother, a steady paycheck and a house of her own were enough of a dream come true; she only hoped it could last.

Almost exactly a year later, on a Monday morning in October, Melle sprung awake before the sun came up, sat up in bed, and said, "Rena, it's late, I've got to get up or I'll lose my job." Then he dropped back on the bed—dead at thirty-one from hope failure. Ten years of wishing, ten years of imagining, ten years of believing, a decade of hoping in the new world of bright hope. Now the pain began for the widow his dead hopes left behind.

Hope can be struck by lightning; but it can also die slowly from repeated slaps of disappointment. Hope hangs on too long sometimes, gets too tired to go on, and has nothing to do but collapse from relentless letdown. Other times the devil's black magic waves a mirage of assurance that our lifetime hope has really come true, and then, with a quick, hard shake of the foundations, whacks it to pieces.

The bigger the dream, the bigger the pain.

Pablo Molenez hoped against hope in his little village of Macua for a chance to get into El Norte, the land of promise for poor Mexicans. A simple dream fired his desire: a steady job, a decent car to drive, and a place of his own to live in. His stubborn heart kept him believing that it was possible.

In the year 1991, he put his total fortune, sixty dollars, into the hands of body smugglers who strapped him to the axle of a station wagon and drove him across the border. He arrived in Los Angeles. He was proud. Took no food stamps. Accepted no welfare. Violated no laws. He found a yard job that paid him in cash, slept on the floor in his sister's apartment, and after living in this luxury for six months, he was sure that his brightest dream had come true.

Then the earth quaked. The apartment house he lived in collapsed. Pablo's sister was killed. He took to the park and hung out there, too stunned to go to work. Police officers questioned him and reported him to the immigration service. The service sent him back to Macua. Pablo no longer hopes to go back to the land of the earthquake.

People who put their hope in God are not spared the heartache of hope failure. As St. Paul observed, when he spoke of the hopes and fears of all the years, all people who hitch their hopes to God are active members of the groan and hope club.[3]

Toward the close of his long and brilliant account of how the tragedies of the twentieth century strangled humanistic optimism to death, Christopher Lasch wondered whether, after optimism passed away, we might be able to discover "a more robust form of hope, which trusts life without denying its tragic character."[4] I shall, in the third section of this book, explore the possibility of such a vigorous hope. But let us not run too fast from the possibilities of pain that hide in the seams of human hope.

Tammy Kramer, one of the lovelier spirits who have blessed my world, was chief of the outpatient AIDS clinic at Los Angeles County Hospital. She was watching a young man who had come in one morning for his regular dose of medicine. He sat in tired silence on a high clinic stool while a new doctor at the clinic poked a needle into his arm and, without looking up at his face, asked, "You are aware, aren't you, that you are not long for this world—a year at most?"

The patient stopped at Tammy's desk on his way out, face distorted in pain, and hissed: "That S.O.B. took away my hope."

"I guess he did. Maybe it's time to find another one."[5]

But is there another?

Just Remember This . . .

Human hoping is always a gamble with pain of the very worst kind. When we pin our happiness on what we hope for, our reward may be the most wretched kind of sadness. Whenever our dearest hopes are crushed, we face this crisis: Do we have a fall-back hope to carry us through the times when the hope we leaned on collapses?

Sum and Substance of Part One

- To hope is human, native to the spirit; we were created to hope just as we were created to think and to feel.
- We hope because we are travelers, people on the way from now to later, from today to tomorrow.
- We need to hope because God gave us the power to imagine the future but gave us no power to control it.
- Hope is conceived by a wish, comes to life with a dream, and is born full term when we believe that the thing we wish for and imagine having is possible for us to have.
- Hope is a spiritual power that keeps us striving to achieve the things we hope for.
- Hope is a spiritual power that keeps us waiting for the things we know we cannot achieve.
- Hope is a spiritual power that survives when the things we hope for are denied us.
- Hope is always shadowed by worry that the good things we imagine may not happen. When we stop hoping, we stop worrying. When we stop worrying, we do not need to hope.
- False hope is, in its many forms, a lie masquerading as a hope.
- When our dearest hopes die, we face the ultimate question of hope: Is there a hope beyond human hoping?

Part Two
How Hopeful People Keep
Their Hope Alive

Chapter 11

✎

HOPEFUL PEOPLE TAKE RESPONSIBILITY FOR THEIR HOPING

A hopeful person is someone who has turned hoping into a habit. In any crisis, she looks for hope the way an artist looks for light. She is predictable; you can coun' on her every time to inject hope into a frightening situatic She has the habit of hoping.

People who have the habit of hope live better than pe who have the habit of despair. They are ever so much ha They respond more effectively to crises. They are stricke not crushed by tragedy. When everything good about life at the foundations and they cannot be sure of what wi pen next, they turn their eyes to the possibility that son good can still come of it. And then they act on the p ties of rescuing some good out of it all. They often do ing for their families, their children, and their friends, the others through the tough times by the infectiou their hopes.

But how do hopeful people manage to keep hope

alive? And how can despairing people get to be more hopeful? The question has no easy answer.

Some people seem to be naturals at hoping.

My wife, Doris, is one of them. Hope is sewn into the seams of her character; she habitually responds to the threat of trouble by focusing on the possibility that bad things may turn out well. In every family crisis that we have faced, including her own bout with cancer, she has grabbed hold of the possibilities for a happy ending and hung on to hope through every fearsome night. Hope has become her style.

I myself have never floated lightly on the swells of hope. My mother taught me early on that bright hopes were the devil's disguise for a proud heart. We who were both humbly sinful and humbly poor were not meant to hope for things beyond what we were given. And most of all we were not meant to hope for much from our own sin-sick souls. So I took it for granted that the odds were stacked against a better life for me.

I have learned a lot about how to counter inherited despair by setting my mind on a faith that better things are possible. It's a tug-of-war, I admit, and my heels are dug in for a long pull before hope has a firm and steady grip on my spirit. In the morning, despair may have the edge. By midday hope may surge back. But I believe that despair will not win the struggle for my soul. Hope will always fight back and in the end prevail because God is on hope's side.

I no longer believe that people who have the habit of hope are tripped into hopefulness by a lucky destiny. I believe that, though their raw materials have made it easier for them, they, too, must choose to hope and to reject despair when they enter early time of trouble. Nor do I believe that people disposed to despair are predestined to hopelessness; they can decide to pit hope against their despair; they can *choose* to hope. This is oversimplified, I know. But it is the truth behind the mystery of how we get to be the sorts of persons we are.

Choosing to keep on struggling against despair and to keep on choosing for hope—this is to take responsibility for our hoping. And accepting responsibility for hope is the beginning of the habit of hopefulness. Once we decide that we are going to write our life story empowered by hope, we can look for and find positive ways of developing the habit of hope, of becoming a more hopeful person and living the productive and courageous and cheerful life that only hopeful people can live.

∽∞∽

Just Remember This . . .

The simple but crucial message of this chapter is that becoming a more hopeful person than we are is up to us. We may be predisposed by our temperament to focus on the bad things that we imagine are coming down the pike. But we are not fated to surrender to our fear of them. We can decide against fear and decide for hope.

Chapter 12

༄

HOPEFUL PEOPLE KNOW
WHAT THEY HOPE FOR

My younger son is what they call an inventory ana-
lyst. He has taught me how important it is to any
productive industry to keep a clear and accurate
account of stock on hand. Imagine the thousands of parts that
go into the making of a car. Then imagine the trouble it would
cost General Motors if no one on the premises had ready access
to precise information about how many of each part were in
stock and where each part was located.

Keeping track of our hopes, I daresay, is even more important than keeping track of nuts and bolts. The blessed—and the
young—have hearts chock-full of hopes. The trouble is that our
hopes get blown around in our spirits like shredded paper thrown
from a window on the tenth floor. They tend to land inside of
our minds where they please, helter-skelter, like things we throw
into a closet when we don't have time to hang them up or sort
them out. So what we have inside of us is such a tangled heap of
hopes that we are not even aware of what our hopes are.

I recommend taking an inventory of our hopes. Please remember that we are concerned only with hopes we currently have in stock. Not the hopes people tell us we *should* have, nor the hopes we *pretend* to have—only the ones we *do* have. Which is to say, we are dealing here only in the things we really wish for, can imagine having, and believe are possible for us to have.

Hopes for what we can be. Each of us hopes to be a better somebody. But being a somebody is to be a galaxy of things, all of them clustered into one person, mixed and shaken down to one complex being. So let me suggest some of the personal qualities that any of us might well hope to acquire.

There are *qualities of character* that some of us hope to have. By this I mean the moral qualities that make for good persons, such as telling the truth even when it costs us something or keeping our promises when breaking them would make life easier for us or taking a stand for what's right even if it is not politically proper.

I suppose that even more of us hope that we can develop better *dispositions,* such as being more cheerful around our kids and having a better sense of humor about each other's borderline lunacy or putting up more graciously with our meddling mothers.

Still more of us hope for personal qualities that could make us more attractive—*aesthetic qualities,* if you will: looking better than we do, maybe losing some weight, or changing hairstyles.

Then there are *qualities of health:* all of us, at some time or another, hope that we can get out of our depression or rid of a nasty cold, gain our old pep back or lose our old back pain, or maybe just feel better about ourselves than we do now.

Hopes for things we do. We all hope to be successful at whatever it is we do. Or do we? I have known a few people who really wished to fail, if only to prove that they did not deserve to succeed, and they were usually quite successful at failing. But down deep, I suspected, even they wished that they could wish to succeed. So I am just assuming we all have some hope of being successful.

Some of us focus our hopes on *success at work*. Some hope for a promotion, others hope to earn more money, most of us hope to be respected for what we do, and some of us just hope to do good work no matter whether anybody notices.

The really lucky among us hope for *success at play*. I envy them. I have friends who carry the torch of hope to every fairway, hoping that one day before they die they will pull their handicaps down by one point. Some people aim their hopes on beating others at their game. Others hope for an early retirement so they have time to dance or travel or go to the theater or collect stamps. I am among those who have next to no hope at all for success at playing; give me a job to accomplish any day.

Some people I know hope to be more *successful at being servants* to others. What they hope for is more time to give a helping hand to people who need it. Or they hope to be more effective at serving others. And some people hope to find the secret of helping hopeless people find hope for themselves.

Hopes for things to own. Life is so full of lovely things and useful things, and the media are so skilled at seducing us into believing that we cannot be happy without them that things are massive items in our hope inventory. We hope for things we do not have now, children or a good friend. We hope for things we already have but want more of, money or power.

And we hope for things we want that are better than what we already have, a better house or a better job.

Hopes for good things to happen to other people. My hopes for my kids are tops on my own hope agenda. And, less often than I like, I also hope for other people's children. Every decent, spirited hoper hopes that poor people will get a fair share of the things that we hope for ourselves. We hope that our friends will do well, not too well, not much better then we do, but still, well enough. Genuine misanthropes may hope that their enemies will suffer a plague, but some of us hope that our enemies will become our friends.

Hopes for good relationships. The one thing most of us hope for most of all, I guess, is to have at least one deeply intimate relationship with someone who loves us. We hope to have close and lasting friendships, happy associations with our grown-up children, and maybe most of all lasting love with our spouses. Sometimes we have to hope that someone will forgive us and become our friend again. Come to think of it, enduring intimate relationships of love are so fragile that we really do need to keep hope alive for keeping them alive. The worst thing that can happen to a withering marriage, for instance, is a loss of hope that it can be revived again.

Hopes for the world. Some people, not all of us, are global hopers. We try to keep hope alive for our physical environment, hope that we can keep it the beautiful and bountiful planet we want our children to live in. Some of us concentrate on hoping for blessings on the hungry and oppressed people of the world—that everyone will one day get a fair share of the things that we already have more of than we can manage. Maybe all of us have some sort of hope that God will come one day and fix the whole world for good.

What I have been trying to do so far is raise our hope awareness so that we at least have a current inventory of our hopes. Now we shall look at our reasons for hoping for what we hope for.

We have, it seems to me, just two basic reasons for hoping for something: we hope to have certain things because they can be the *means* of getting something else that we hope for, and we hope for things simply for their own sake—as *ends in themselves.*

Most of our hopes are *means hopes.* We hope mostly for things that we believe will bring us something else. Money is the simplest example. A shriveled soul may hope for a lot of money simply to enjoy counting it; most of us hope to have money so that we can use it to get the better things we hope for.

We also hope for things as *ends in themselves.* We want them for their own sakes, not as a means of getting something else. The simplest example is happiness. Does anyone want to be happy so that he can do better on the job or be a better lover or be more healthy? Isn't it quite the other way around? Don't we hope to be healthy and wealthy and wise because we believe that these things will make us happier or more blessed than we are?

We are not always sure whether the things we hope for are means of making still other hopes come true or whether they are what we want for their very own sakes. Why do you hope for a good education for your children? Or for more beauty in your life? Or for love and friendship? Or for getting closer to God? Are these means or ends? Nobody knows but you.

Once again, let me explain the point of all this: we need to know what we hope for because our hopes are too important to leave in a jumbled heap like a basket of unsorted laundry.

Think of the mess you would be in if you were doing a large job on your computer and you never created any files to put your documents in. We are in a much worse mess if we have no mental inventory of our hopes. We all tend to become what we most hope for, so taking inventory of our hopes is a way of taking inventory of our future selves.

One thing is sure: we have to do *our own* inventory. Nobody else can tell us what we really *do* hope for or *why* we hope for them. Others may tell us what we *ought* to hope for. But only we can know what we actually *do* hope for.

❦

Just Remember This . . .

> *Hoping is the main business of the human spirit. To do it successfully, we need to keep tabs on what it is we hope for and the reasons why we hope for the things we do; we should know the reasons we want them so much and why we will be deeply disappointed if they crash on us before they have a chance to come true. Keeping hope alive inside of us is the most important gift we can give ourselves. The first step is to know what it is that we hope for and why we hope for it.*

Chapter 13

༄

HOPEFUL PEOPLE KNOW
WHICH HOPES MATTER MOST

When some hopes fail us, we fret. When others fail us, we grieve. But we all carry a few hopes in our breasts that, if they crash, we are crushed. Hope's pendulum swings from a moment's pleasure to an eternity's joy. But we always invest something of our happiness in every hope we hope.

The danger is that we may get what we hope for and then discover it did not give us the dividend that we expected from it. And it is easy to invest so much of ourselves that when our hopes do not come true we are far more than disappointed, we are devastated. The smarter we are about how much we invest in our hopes, the more pain we can spare ourselves.

In this chapter, then, we will look at ways to *rank* our hopes. We should rank them according to how much they will affect our well-being if they do or do not come true. I do not intend to tell you how much of your happiness you *should* invest in one or another of your hopes. My aim is only to suggest a way of becoming more conscious of how much you are already invested in your various hopes.

I suggest ranking our hope involvement under three main categories: preference hopes, vital hopes, and fall-back hopes.

Preference Hopes

We flip the word *hope* off our tongues several times a day to refer to anything that we want to happen but cannot be sure it will. Such as hoping it won't rain on my golf game next Saturday. Or that the soufflé I am making for dinner for my husband's mother will not collapse. Or that I can get home before the kids get there. Or that my daughter will get into law school. Or maybe marry the man she loves and start a family instead.

For me, these are preference hopes. I prefer that they come true, but I do not expect them to make or break me if they do not come true. I may be disappointed, yes, but getting or losing them is not vital to whether my life is going to be worth the living.

Vital Hopes

Vital hopes are hopes of a very different breed. They are hopes that promise to bring us serious benefits for our very being if they come true—and serious personal loss if they don't. They are vital to us because they can mean the difference between happiness and sadness, maybe even life and death of the spirit.

What might be a vital hope to you? That your children will grow up healthy and good and useful to humankind? That you will live awhile longer and stay well enough to do some creative work or have some interesting fun when you get old?

That you will have enough money to keep your children from worrying about you? That your wife's mastectomy will clean out all of her cancer? I am only making suggestions. The point is that if you believe that getting or not getting what you hope for is crucial to your very well-being, your hope is a vital hope.

Let me try a simple example to illustrate the difference between a preference hope and a vital hope.

One day Doris discovered that my new white shirt had a big, blue blotch on the front of it from a leaky ballpoint pen I had carried in my shirt pocket on a flight from Chicago. Miffed a notch or two beyond what I thought a spoiled shirt really rated, she huffed, "Well, I certainly hope I can get the stain out." But neither she nor I suffered any serious loss to our comfort in life when she was not able to make this hope come true.

A few days later, Doris came home from her doctor's office with word that she might have cancer again, another kind this time.

"Oh, God, I hope not!"

A vital hope for sure. Both of us were invested to the hilt. She had had cancer before, and we desperately did not want her to have it again. We put our vital hopes where our hearts are. (As it turned out, thank God, she did not have it.)

Fall-back Hopes

When we hope for something that we want more than anything in the world and that something is taken away from us, we need a fall-back hope.

A fall-back hope is not a plan B hope to replace the hope we lost. Not like a hope of winning Jane after you have given up hope on Nancy. It is a hope that supports *all* our other living hopes and still survives when those hopes die.

Sometimes our minds get so packed with vital hopes that we have no space for a fall-back hope. Why bother our heads with a nebulous religious hope when we already have too many hopes, specific and expensive, to work on—hopes for our children's education, our retirement, our marriage. Then on some desolate morning the one vital hope that we have counted on most to give us the happiness we want is ripped out of our lives. We hold our dead hope in our arms. Our life is as good as finished; we will never smile again.

Then, in the sinkhole of our grief for the loss of that one most vital hope, we may be given another hope. We cannot explain it. We can't even express it. Only a child knows how. But it is suddenly the most real hope we have ever had. Not a sappy sympathy text of hope that everything is for the best. Not even a hope to replace the hope we lost. But still a hope as real as our sadness, and a hope as truly our own as our tears were our own, a hope that in spite of its stabbing cruelty, our life is blessed.

Maybe a story will make my point concrete.

A friend of mine put all his hope eggs in one basket—in his son, Sam, who looked and smelled like a boy bound to do his daddy proud. My friend worried a lot, though, because he thought Sam rode his Harley in a devil-may-care sort of way that could not forever beat the odds against calamity. Well, horrendously, Sam did crash his bike, rammed it into a freeway abutment one clear night.

At the hospital the medics in the trauma center attached him to a respirator to keep him breathing, but then discovered that, though the blood ran warm through his veins, the thinking part of his brain was dead. The medic in charge, who knew my friend well, found him in the waiting room and said, "I'm afraid that there is no hope for Sam. But there *is* hope."

Odd thing for a doctor to say. What could he have meant? Did he mean to soften my friend's blow by reminding him that the real Sam was alive in heaven, even when his buckled body sprawled twisted on the 210? I do not think so. He was not talking about a hope *for* something that could compensate for Sam's dying.

Not a hope *for* anything in particular, but a hope *in* Someone in particular. At such a time, one's hope becomes one's trust—a trust in Someone who gives us a reason to keep hoping that even a life spiked with grief can be a life lived in gratitude.

We can get a fix on our own fall-back hope by asking ourselves this question: If I lost all hope of keeping or getting the one thing that I thought I needed to make my life worth living, would I discover that, after all, I had a good reason to keep hoping that I could still find some joy in living? If you have such a hope, it is your fall-back hope. Now you are not hoping for some*thing* to replace what you had hoped for and lost. Now you are investing your hope *in* something or somebody who you hope will hold you up and keep you going on the way to whatever future is meant for you.

You have probably noticed that I have not tried to tell you which of your hopes should be only preferences and which of your hopes should be truly vital to you. Nor have I told you what your fall-back hope, your hope-in-the-hole, should be. At this point, I want only to help you to be more aware of your portfolio of hopes.

⋙

Just Remember This . . .

> *Not all hopes are equal. Some of our hopes are much more important to us than others. Some hopes we can shed without much loss. Other hopes, when we lose them, cost us almost as much as life itself. Still others—our fall-back hopes—are the life supports for all our other hoping. They are our hope beyond hope. Our fall-back hope.*

Chapter 14

Hopeful People Adjust Old Hopes to New Realities

There was an old cavalry motto that went like this: "When your horse dies, dismount and saddle another." To that good horse sense, I would add a piece of hope sense: When a hope dies, let it go, and saddle another.

Hope does not have to die when hopes die. It only needs to be readjusted to fit the new reality that the death of one hope left us with. Call it "hope adjustment"—getting old hopes in sync with new reality.

I suppose you could say that this is what my mother did when my father fell back dead on his pillow that hope-killing Monday morning. While he was alive, my mother could live off crumbs of hope from my father's table. But when he left, her secondhand hopes died with him.

Her new reality was that at age thirty she was alone in a strange and loveless land with five small kids to feed and no job skills to earn the money to feed them with. The New Deal and public welfare were eleven years away. She understood

English little and spoke it less. She had no kin, not a cousin or an aunt or a distant uncle, on the continent; the only people she had were a couple of upright neighbors whose Christian counsel to her was that she should give two or three of her children away. This was her new reality.

Did she have any hope left to adjust to her reality? Not many hopes. But hope? Yes, she had one.

Every night, when she had finally gotten us all to bed and all the lights were out, she would get on her knees in front of a wobbly kitchen chair and trouble deaf heaven with her boot-less Frisian cries. I slept in a small room within easy earshot of the kitchen, and I waited for her parting petition, which was the same every night. She named each of us, beginning with Jessie, the oldest, running down through Peter, Catherine, and Wesley, all spoken in Frisian, and, after an eternity's intermezzo, mine—Lubbert—at the tail end, as if she were holding all of us kids up for God to see what He had left her with. Especially me. My name, I thought, did not drop from her mouth as the last syllable of a series, it sounded more as if she were blow-ing it out to make sure it got up to Him. When, night after night, I heard my name being blown off to heaven, it gradu-ally dawned on me that I was stuck with God for life.

Saturday nights were toughest; they were the nights when, after doing the whole week's chores in one day—without ben-efit of a gas stove, bathtub, telephone, or hot tap water—she had to get us all scrubbed for the Lord's Day. Sometimes, done in and at her wit's end, she would leave the five of us squab-bling and whining in the kitchen and closet herself in the bath-room, sit on the toilet seat—a flushing toilet being our only bathroom convenience—bury her face in her wet apron, and slowly rock back and forth. On the forward swing she would bawl in wordless heaves, and on the back swing she'd suck in an unbelievably long breath for the next heave.

The five of us didn't know what to say to each other. We stood around gangling, dumb, giggling some, ashamed; I looked at her through the keyhole and wished I dared to cry. Then my sister Catherine would relieve our clammy guilt by shrugging it all off with: "Ma is having her Saturday night fit again." We giggled. A child's cruelty? I don't think so. It was the only way we could lift the unbearable burden of being the cause of our mother's despair.

In the vacuum of God's terrible silence, in the emptiness of her lonesome abandonment, she was reducing all the hopes that she had borrowed from my father to this one, open-ended, fall-back hope—hope that God would come, hold her up, and keep her going. My mother, I have come to think, was adjusting her share of my father's big hopes for big things to her own hoping for almost nothing at all. But the adjustment was not so much from hoping for big things to hoping for small ones. The adjustment was from hoping *for* things *from* God to throwing herself *on* the lap of God—just to keep some mustard seed of hope alive.

Life is a series of hope adjustments. To let old hopes fade away, like old soldiers, and to settle on new ones—this is to grow up as a human being in a world that can grind any hope to dust.

If our hopes of having a nest full of children died from acute infertility, we can adjust our hopes to fit other children we love, children we adopt or children we teach. If our hope that our children would be stars that lit up the sky died when it became clear that they were able only to light a small candle, we can adjust our hope to the possibility that they may light up one small nook of their small world.

Getting old is prime time for hope adjustment. As we creep into the geriatric stage, we begin to accept the fact that many of our highest hopes are not going to be realized, at least not in time for us to see them. So we lower the level and narrow the gauge of our active hopes, and leave the unfulfilled big ones with God. Our hopes also get more self-centered and body driven. Decrepitude is not a spiritual adventure. Every new insult to our body yanks our hope earthward.

For instance, I forgot what I ate for dinner at Lozano's three nights ago and I hope I'm not getting Alzheimer's. I've been getting up more often at night these days and I hope that I'm not due for prostate cancer. Street signs are getting harder to read, so I hope I'm not going blind. I have even begun to hope that death will be gentle when it comes for Doris and she hopes the same for me. And though we both hope to go to heaven when we die, we also hope the Lord feels no urgency about getting us there.

Make no mistake about it, our hopes do not become more spiritual just because we are getting closer to the time for discarding our bodies. And yet, I find that my hope mellows some with age; my early discontent with the way things were is melting down to gratitude for the way things are. I am sometimes stunned by how much better my life is than I once dared hope it would be. And I find myself (bit by bit) adjusting my earlier hopes that were born of discontent with the way things were to a more serene hope that I will be content at last with whatever God wills to give.

⌘

Just Remember This . . .

> *Life is a continued story of hope adjustment. Things change. Hopes die. But hope does not have to die—not ever. And it will not die if we are mature enough, brave enough, and if we believe enough to readjust our hopes to the new reality we are jammed into every time another hope dies.*

Chapter 15

⟡

HOPEFUL PEOPLE REMEMBER THE GOOD TIMES—AND THE BAD

P eople often think that hope thrives only on visions of good things tucked behind the curtain of the future, like a prisoner's hope of getting out one day when life will really begin. But actually hope feeds on memory. Memories of hopes that came true. And memories of horrors that we survived.

This is the insight that led the Simon Wiesenthal Foundation to adopt this sentence as its motto: "Hope lives when people remember." Even when what people remember is awful. Recall that the Wiesenthal Foundation is dedicated to keeping our memory linked with the worst things that human beings have ever done to other human beings.

A survivor of Auschwitz told me that every now and then he takes his grandchildren with him to revisit the site of the death camp. Why? To keep his hate alive? To make sure his grandchildren hate the people who did this to him? Not for either of these reasons. He goes back to show his grandchildren the miracle of his survival. To let his grandchildren know that men are capable of horrible evil. And to move them early on to hope that they will do great good instead.

We would not hope for goodness if we did not know evil. We would live in the illusion that the way things are is the way they are supposed to be. And we would feel no need to hope that they could ever get to be the way they are supposed to be. So each time we remember the evil that was, we also face up to the evil that can fall on us again, and we are moved to hope that good will come instead. So even a visit to Auschwitz can keep hope alive.

This is the mood in which Jewish believers keep the holy days. Rabbi Yechiel Eckstein recalls that even the "blackest, most sorrowful day in the Jewish year"—the fast of *Tisha b'Av* in which Jews mourn the destruction of the temple and the brutal martyrdom of Jews through the years—"is injected with a note of hope. . . . In the afternoon we rise from our lowly mourning stools and recall . . . that the Messiah will be born on Tisha b'Av . . . [and that] redemption will sprout forth from the very depths of suffering and despair."[1]

Christians celebrate the death of Jesus in the Lord's Supper to remember that He died on the cross for the sins of the world. But the supper does not end with the recollection of suffering. We listen to the Lord telling His disciples to repeat this same memorial until He returns. Listening, we rekindle our hope that He will indeed return and that, when He does, God will make His world work right again for everyone. That He will see to it that, once and for all, all will be well with the world and all will be well with all of His children.

Now I want to turn from the memory of great tragedies to the memory of small triumphs.

As I mentioned earlier, when my father—and his hopes with him—died, my mother could only fall back on her fall-back hope. She had had enough of pipe dreams. But as long as she had God to fall back on, she was able to keep a few small hopes alive.

One of her abiding hopes was for a warm house for her children during the long Michigan winter. She worried about the winter because she could never be sure she would have enough money to buy a winter's supply of coal. She also worried about the winter because she was never sure that when the tax man came in January she would have enough money to keep our house out of his hands. These were her never-ending worries, so they became her two never-ending hopes.

The day the coal man backed his rattletrap Mack truck up against the casement of our coal cellar window and shoveled a ton of the cheapest, dustiest hunks of coal down the chute, my mother set herself down at the kitchen table and said, "See so, there, we have it again. Don't I always tell you that God takes care of widows?" When she had trudged the icy sidewalks downtown to the city hall and slid an envelope with her sixty-two dollars in it across the counter and then walked back home again, she would sit down and, in the tones set aside for announcing great truth, say to us: "See so, there, we have it again. Don't I always tell you that God takes care of widows?"

I remember. And the memory feeds my hopes.

"Count your blessings," went an old gospel song that we sang a lot during the Great Depression, "name them one by one. Count your many blessings, see what God has done." For too long, I thought life was too tough to be tenderized by such simple blue-sky piety. Now I know by experience that counting the blessings I remember is the surest way to keep alive hope for blessings still to come.

I recall Benjamin Weir and how he kept his hope alive while he was a hostage in Lebanon and blessings came one by one, in small packages that were not always easy to spot.

"How did you spend your time during all those months?" reporters asked him after he was released.

"Counting my blessings."

"Your blessings?"

"Yes, some days I got to take a shower. Sometimes there were some vegetables in my food. And I could always be thankful for the love of my family."

Counting blessings was Weir's secret defense against demon despair. And remembering this day's special blessings in the frame of last month's special miseries was a reinforcement for hope of bigger blessings to come.

As I have slowly crept into decrepitude, I have been surprised at how often I feel washed in warm waves of awe at the graces of life. They come over me when my wife and I sit down to supper and we start counting the blessings we have been given that day. The deeper my wonder at the gift of a day almost gone, the stronger my hope becomes for the one on the way. And the brighter my memory of the gifts of good days, the stronger may be my hope in the dark days on the way.

No one can be expected to hope for a better future who does not have some memories of hopes that came true in his past. Without any good memories to feed from, hope eventually starves to death. There are swarms of cold-eyed young men and empty-eyed young women roving the jungles of the city who, if you told them that there was hope for them, would spit in your face. They need some good to remember or they will never hope for good to come or even have hope of having hope.

So I need to conclude with two sober thoughts. No one has a right to count his own blessings without doing something to give others some blessings to count. And no one has a right to hope for good things for herself unless she hopes for good things to come to others.

∝∾

Just Remember This . . .

> *A person who has the habit of hope also has the habit of remembering. Hope needs memories the way a writer needs notes. This is partly because hope depends so much on imagination; our images of the future are sweepings from our remembrances of things past. If we expect to keep hope alive we need to keep memory alive: happy memories of good things we hoped for that were fulfilled; grateful memories of bad things we survived.*

Chapter 16

❦

HOPEFUL PEOPLE WATCH FOR SIGNS

We need to keep our eyes open for signs that things can get better than they are. Not just for us, but for other people, particularly people living on the edge of despair. What we must remember, though, is that a sign just says that there is hope, not that what we hope for is certain to happen.

Anything can be a sign. If it points us away from itself to something we want to find, it is a sign to us. The way a banged-up board on the side of a road points us to the town we want to spend the night in.

In the year 1932, with the country buried deep in depression, Franklin Roosevelt flashed a smile that became a sign of hope to a people worn out with worry. "People drew strength from the very cock of his head, the angle of his cigarette holder, the trademark grin that was a semaphore of hope."[1] The people mired in fear were not looking for presidential grins. They were looking for jobs. But when they saw the confident grin of FDR and heard him say that the only thing they had to fear was fear, they saw a sign that better times were coming.

My current favorite sign of hope is what a former student of mine has done for abused and abandoned children of Los Angeles.

A brief background: The county of Los Angeles has on its hands a steady flow of more than 70,000 abused and abandoned children. More than enough to pack Dodger Stadium. These are children the child welfare agency has scooped up from parents who have beaten them, starved them, drugged them, or abandoned them. The scooping goes on nonstop.

Once the children are rescued from their parents, they are jammed into a bleak, overcrowded institution where a staff too small to care for them all keeps them in custody until they are shuttled to the first of the perpetually revolving doors of a foster care system that is out of control. "Kids of the system" they call themselves when they get bigger, by which they mean "the hopeless kids."

The name on my hope sign is Mary Rotzien. I came to know her when she was plowing doggedly towards her doctor's degree in psychology and doing her internship at the county institution I mentioned earlier. Mary Rotzien refused to believe that abused children *had* to be treated like a tide of flotsam from a polluted sea. She knew somehow that she was, then and there, being called to find a better way.

She applied to foundations for grants and got a few small ones. She talked to every congregation that would listen to her plea for families who would commit themselves to long-term foster care of high-risk children. She and her husband, Brian, who had caught her hope, cleaned out their garage, turned it into a headquarters, and with some of the grant money hired a part-time professional person to get the work started. They called it Child-SHARE, an acronym for *Shelter Homes—A Rescue Effort.*

As I write, more than four hundred badly wounded children are in the care of licensed Child-SHARE parents. These foster parents are backed up by other parents—also trained by Child-SHARE—who relieve the foster parents when they need a respite. All of the parents were recruited from a network of 250 supportive Los Angeles churches.

By the end of next year a good number of those children will have been adopted by their foster parents, and most of the others will stay with their foster families as long as it takes for their parents to get themselves in shape to care for them. Child-SHARE parents have achieved an unparalleled record of faithfulness to the children they care for, a record that no government agency in the country comes close to matching.

Mary Rotzien and Child-SHARE have no illusions of rescuing all the abused kids of Los Angeles County. But they have hoisted a bright sign of hope. And to those with eyes to see it, the sign says that if this much can be done by a few, more can be done by many.

Habitat for Humanity is not solving the problems of homeless people in America. But is not every house it builds or rebuilds a sign of hope that the problem could be solved? World Vision does not expect to feed every hungry stomach or heal every wound in the world. But with every stomach it does feed and every wound it does heal, it posts a sign that says: there is hope that one day every stomach will be fed and every wound healed. My friend Dr. Kevin Lake devotes a good share of his time to helping out at a primitive little hospital in Haiti; he has no pipe dreams about healing the sickness of that sad island. But he, too, is putting up a sign that reads: there is hope.

Signs of hope in smaller scope are everywhere. One teenager gets off drugs and comes home. A neighbor gets retrained and finds a new job in hard times. A woman whose pregnancy is a worry refuses to have an abortion. A new shelter for the homeless is up and serving. A scrapping couple forgive each other and start over. A handicapped child takes one step.

All signs. Not solutions, but pointers to hope for solutions. And if we keep our eyes open, we will find them. A mere baby, after all, lying in a manger long ago is still a sign of hope that the Creator has joined His earth and is heaven-bent on fixing it.

∞

Just Remember This . . .

We need to watch for signs that bad things could get better. Sometimes the signs are as bright as a falling star against a black sky. Sometimes the signs are subtle, like the tracks of a fawn in a dark green forest. They are there, traces and tokens, that hint to us that things can be better than most people believe they can.

Chapter 17

⌒∞⌒

HOPEFUL PEOPLE MAKE
REGULAR REALITY CHECKS

Puff on pipe dreams and you get the smoke of illusion. Sniff illusion and you get the first whiff of hopelessness. Hope needs to stay clear of illusions and stay on track with reality—not confined by reality but not out of touch with it either. This is why we need to make an occasional reality check on our hope.

Let me suggest a few checkpoints.

Am I actually hoping for this or do I only think I ought to hope for it?

Preachers are forever reminding believers like me that God promises us some wonderful things which we *ought* to hope for. The burden of knowing we *ought* to hope for them tempts us to pretend that we really *do* hope for the things we are *supposed* to hope for. We sing old gospel songs of hope like "Standing on the Promises" even though our hearts are frozen by fear into a lump of despair. We read Bible passages about being born again to a living hope while hope floats dead in the swamp of our aching spirits. We get into such a habit of using the vocabulary of hope without ever experiencing the power of hope that we lose touch with what is real and what is pretend in our hoping.

So maybe a reality check on hope is especially vital for religious people. But religious or not, we all need to ask ourselves: Do we really wish for the good things we say we hope for, and do we really believe that they are possible?

Do I hope for it or am I only curious about it?

Everybody likes to have inside information on how things are going to shape up in world affairs on the way to the world's end. But curiosity about what is going to happen is not the same as hoping that it will. Not even when we feed our curiosity on ancient biblical predictions tailored to our times by imaginative interpreters.

Do I have a sound reason for believing that what I hope for is possible?

We need more than a wish and a dream to support our hope. We need sound reasons for believing that the things we wish for and dream about are possible. People who want to be more hopeful need a nose for the difference between reasonable hope and pipe-dream smoke.

Do I get enough sleep?

Sometimes what hope needs most is a good night's sleep. Sleep-deprived people are inclined to be hope-deprived people. So a check on our sleep habits is at the same time a reality check on hope. For some of us, the way back to hope is the way back to bed.

Is my body's chemistry in balance?

Chronic hopelessness comes with chronic depression just as chronic depression comes with chronic hopelessness. When the two of them hitch up, they drag us down into the darkest valley of dark despair. And the cause may be, not a failing of the spirit, but a rogue chemical in our biosystem. When this is what is going on, the way back to the light may be a prudent prescription of well-tested chemicals.

Am I in touch with how much my hopes mean to my life?

Do I know which of my hopes are vital to my life? And which are no more than preferences? Do I know which of my hopes I hang on to because if they come true my life will be affected right to the core? And do I know which hopes I can let go because if they don't come true their loss would be no calamity for me even if it made life a little less comfortable?

Do I know what my fall-back hope is?

Do I have one hope that will survive the crash of all my other hopes? A hope that can look three-dimensional tragedy full in the face and not quit? And do I know what that hope is?

Making reality checks on our hopes is simply a way of keeping in touch with our hopes. The key word here is *our*. We are talking about our own very real hopes. Not what we tell ourselves we should hope for. But what we actually do hope for—what we wish for, what we imagine having, and what we have reason to believe *can* happen.

∞

Just Remember This . . .

To keep hope real, we need to make regular reality checks. Here are the checkpoints: Do I hope or do I believe I ought to hope? Do I have hope for the future or only a curiosity about the future? Do I have reason to believe that what I hope for is really possible? Do I get enough sleep? Do I need medication for the depression that smothers my hope? Do I know which of my hopes matter most? Do I know what my fall-back hope is?

Chapter 18

❦

HOPEFUL PEOPLE LET OTHERS DO THEIR HOPING FOR THEM

Hope is catching. It is a fine grace to have someone near who will keep on hoping for us when our hopes fall into a deep sleep. Substitute hopers can keep hope alive until our own hopes have a revival.

The best gift parents can give a dispirited and despairing child is to give him clear signals that *they* hope *for* him. The best thing a friend can do for a despairing friend is to be her vicarious hoper. The best therapy begins when a client who has lost hope in himself is convinced that his therapist has hope for him. The best church we can belong to is one that not only preaches hope for the world, but demonstrates to us that it has hope for us.

It is at this point that we discover how tightly hope is knit to trust. I know that anyone who trusts me has hope for me. I also know that someone's trust in me ignites my own trust in myself and then my trust gives new life to my hope.

I want to relate two personal experiences. In the first one,

I failed to trust someone and my failure cost him (I fear) some loss of hope for himself. In the second one, someone important to me trusted me and gave me hope for myself. First, *mea culpa*. And then my tribute.

I was slobbering to a friend about the pain that one of my children was suffering at the time, and she responded by telling me that my trouble was that I did not have enough trust.

"What does that have to do with my son's pain?"

"You don't trust him to suffer. You don't trust any of your children to suffer. You have done your share, for heaven's sake, and you survived, why don't you trust them to suffer and survive?"

She had me. I was one of those tender-love parents who think they love their children too much to let them suffer pain. I realize now that I was actually hurting them by trying to shield them from pain. They surely sensed that if I could not trust them to suffer, I must have lacked trust in their characters. Which, in turn, signaled to them that I did not have much hope that they would be strong enough to survive the hard times on their own. My signal said to them: You are incompetents when it comes to pain. And if I could not trust them and if I lacked hope for them, I siphoned off their trust in and their hope for themselves.

Now the other experience.

Thirty years ago, as time pushed me across the border of fifty, circumstances combined to lead me into a job as professor of ethics at Fuller Seminary, the largest graduate theological school in the world. I had never taught ethics in my life, and I was not at all sure that I was up to the job; in fact, I "knew" I wasn't. But I also knew that I was the only available candidate.

The president of Fuller, the late David Hubbard, had rigorous expectations of scholarly publications from his faculty. After I had been at the complicated field of ethics for just a few years, I had no hope of contributing anything interesting let alone scholarly to the guild of fellow scholars.

I figured that—what with his expectations of me—my president deserved to know my doubts. So I told him. I said that after three years of teaching ethics, I had no hope of making the kind of scholarly contribution that he had assumed I would. I might instead, I told him, be able to write something that would be helpful to people like my pastor or my Aunt Sophie. Hubbard wasted no breath trying to convince me that I really could do the scholarly stuff if I put my mind to it. Instead, he said, "Lew, I know you, and I know that whatever you do best will serve everyone else best."

That was all he said. But I *heard* him say, "I trust you." His trust in me exposed his hope for me. And *his* hope gave *me* hope because I respected him enough to trust his trust in me.

In the latest of his uncommonly wise books, Max DePree remarks that: "Trust begins with a personal commitment to respect others."[1] This means that if someone is going to trust me he has to respect me first. But it also means that I need to respect the person who trusts me before I can trust his trust.

My brother-in-law Douglas Hall, an uncommon lawyer with an uncommon passion for the weak and the poor whom justice commonly forgets, is an artist at trusting people in ways that make them strive to be worthy of his trust. Doug devoted the best part of his career to defending poor people who could not afford an attorney. He retired a few years ago and was given a splendid send-off at a big dinner in his honor. One of the speakers was a federal judge, a stately looking, middle-aged black man. The judge recalled how Doug's trust in him had given him hope and how his own hope for himself had salvaged his life. I recall Mary, Doug's wife, telling me what the judge said:

> I was a hopeless kid, on trial for a felony, and I was convicted. But the judge surprised everybody by putting me on probation in custody of my own attorney. I asked my attorney to tell me what he wanted me to do. He said that he wanted me to do whatever I wanted to do. I said that I needed him to tell me what to do. He said that he trusted me to take responsibility for myself and do the right thing on my own. I said that I wasn't ready to be on my own, that I would probably go right back to the same tricks. He said that that was a choice I would have to make. I *begged* him to tell me what to do. He said he trusted me, and that was that.
>
> I didn't know what to make of him; nobody had ever respected me that much. But I decided that if a man like Douglas Hall could trust me to make my own decisions, there must be some hope for me. So I grabbed hold of the hope and here I am.

Respect begets trust. Trust begets hope. Hope begets redemption.

⧡

Just Remember This . . .

Disabled hopers need someone to give them a hope break.

Someone to take over for us until we get the bugs out of our hope. Everybody needs somebody who can be a vicarious hoper. This is why hope survives best in a community of hope. We know people have hope for us when we know they trust us. And if we respect them enough to believe their trust, we gain new hope for ourselves.

Chapter 19

⁂

HOPEFUL PEOPLE GET HOPE FOR A GOOD FUTURE BY FORGIVING A BAD PAST

I n a world like ours, where people hurt each other badly
and wrong each other in the bargain, we can get ourselves
stuck forever to a bad past that steals away our hope for
a better future. The memory of how a trusted friend or spouse
or parent violated our trust can so mesmerize our spirits that
it locks our minds to the memory. And as long as we are hostage
to the memory, we are not free to hope.

Memory, as I have said, is a resource for hope, but first it
needs to be leeched of the poison of hate. Life offers only one
way to drain the hate and replace it with hope. Once wounded
and wronged, our way back into hope for the future is the way
out of the bilge of bitterness about the past—a way paved by
forgiveness.

We must forgive the other person. Then, we must forgive
ourselves.

Let's talk about forgiving other people first. If someone
has done serious wrong to us, we simply cannot go on in a

relationship of trust with him unless something is done to undo the wrong. The wrong of it more than the pain of it builds a wall between us. Either the person who wronged us must do something to right the wrong, or we, the victims, must forgive him for what he did. Otherwise there is no hope for our relationship.

Forgiving is a minor miracle, a bloodless surgery we perform on our spirits. It goes like this, though not necessarily in this order: (1) We begin to see the offender as a flawed human being, not a devil, but a blemished person not all that much different from ourselves. (2) We surrender our precious right to get even with him, and choose to live with the scales unbalanced. (3) We gradually, oh so gradually, find the will to wish him well.

These are the three basic steps of every act of forgiveness. Once begun—and remember that it is almost always a process, sometimes a lifelong journey—we are open to whatever our future holds. We have hope again. People who discover the grace to forgive almost always discover the grace of hope besides.[1]

It is important to remember that hope-giving forgiveness happens totally inside the victim who does the forgiving. It gives us hope for a reconciliation with the person who wronged us. But it gives no guarantee of it. And it certainly involves no obligation to go back to him.

The good news is that even if we cannot be reconciled to the other person, we have by forgiving him created hope for ourselves. Every time we forgive, we set a prisoner free, and the prisoner we set free is ourselves. Free to hope again.

Now, let's take a look at how we forgive ourselves.

People often tell me that forgiving themselves is harder

than forgiving other people. I think they are right. But we make it harder for ourselves by confusing the act of forgiving ourselves with the ability to accept ourselves (or approve of ourselves). We forgive ourselves for *things we do*. We accept ourselves for the *persons we are*.

The distinction is absolutely crucial. Nobody can forgive herself for the sort of person she *is*; she can forgive herself only for the sorts of things she has done. On the other hand, if we are able to accept ourselves we gain the freedom to forgive ourselves as well. For no one can forgive herself for a bad thing she *did* unless she can also accept herself for what she is.

Take me for instance. As I grew up I "knew" for sure that I was a wholly unacceptable creature. In fact, a quite disgusting one. How could a thirteen-year-old boy of six feet with only 120 pounds of flesh on his bones, who looked for sure like a walking case of terminal rickets, couldn't hit a baseball for trying, and, besides, thought naughty thoughts and had naughty dreams every other night, how could he, I ask you, be anything but a hopeless case? I found no reason at all to suppose that on anybody's scale, especially God's, there might be enough good in me to come even close to where I could accept or approve of myself. So I set out, as most people in my condition do, consciously or not, to see to my own failure.

Why should I try to succeed when I knew I did not have enough good in me to give me any hope of succeeding? So I failed in almost everything. And my failures gave me added proof that I was hopeless. Anything I was guilty of *doing* only added weight to my unrelieved judgment on the hopeless sort of secret creep I *was*.

I learned, later on, that I was after all, in spite of my doubts, capable of some success. I succeeded fairly well at college, once

I got the tardy nerve to go there, and at graduate school and then as a minister of the gospel and a teacher and writer. I wondered why my success at what I *did* was never enough to convince me that I was acceptable for what I *was*. For every success that I achieved, I found ten spiritual blemishes inside of my own soul to condemn myself for.

Even while I became rather expert at telling other people about how the Maker of the Universe freely accepts the unacceptable, I felt so inwardly unacceptable that deep in my gut I did not really believe that the grace of God applied to me. Thus I was doubly unacceptable; besides everything else that was ugly about me, I was a hypocrite. And I knew for sure that there is no hope at all for hypocrites.

Later, embarrassingly later, I was, on a certain Tuesday, seized, possessed, overwhelmed by the grace of God's unconditional acceptance. It came to me so powerfully that I could feel it, taste it, ingest it, roll in it, romp in it, rest in it. It took a huge gulp, an overdose of grace, to shock me into total awareness of this paradoxical miracle. I could be unacceptable to every critic on earth as well as to myself, but, no matter, I *was* accepted. The only relevant question left for me was whether I had the humility to accept my acceptance by God without any regard to whether I was acceptable to anyone else.

When I accepted the grace that accepted me, I had the grace to accept myself as well. And when I accepted as the deepest truth about myself that nothing I could ever become in the future could get God to reject me, I gained hope for myself. And whenever I lose my hold on grace, as I do from time to time, I lose my hold on hope for myself. For me, the key of grace opens the door to hope.

So much for accepting myself. What has it to do with forgiving myself? This: Once I accepted myself for what I *was*, I was prepared to forgive myself for things I had *done*. Once we know that nothing we have ever done can get God to reject us because of what we are, we feel free to forgive ourselves for whatever we have *done*. When God accepts us for what we *are*, who are we not to forgive ourselves for what we have *done*? And each time we do forgive ourselves we pull our feet out of yesterday's failure and begin to hope again for tomorrow's blessing.

∽◎∾

Just Remember This . . .

One way to lose hope for a good future is to be stuck to a bad past. One way to find hope is to forgive the past. To forgive is to unglue ourselves from bad things people did to us yesterday. And to free ourselves from the bad things we did to others—or ourselves. Becoming a more forgiving person always, not sometimes, but always, turns us into a more hopeful person.

Chapter 20

❦

HOPEFUL PEOPLE LIVE BY FAITH, NOT BY FATE

Whenever someone invites me to go fishing, I warn him that there are no fish in the sea the day I throw out a line. I am fated not to catch fish. If I were a master fisherman and owned all the fancy fisherman's lures and had all knowledge of where the fish were and when they were biting, I still would not catch any. God's plan for my life does not include catching fish.

Mind you, I do not believe in fate. I hate fate. But I do have an attitude, maybe a feeling of fate, about certain things. Fatalism about fishing is just one of them. And it troubles me more than a little that I sometimes carry my fatalism about fishing into the serious places of my life. I am troubled because when I feel I am fated not to do good things, I lose hope that I can.

To live by fate is to persist in the feeling that whatever is destined to happen will happen no matter what we do to avoid it. (Remember, we are talking about *attitude* here, not theory.) The feeling of being fated comes in several guises, and we give

113

them several names. But they all have this in common: they leave us poor in hope.

Shame. We are too flawed inside to be worthy of the good things that better people hope for. If we were not so hopelessly flawed we, too, might have hope. But there is no hope for such unworthy lumps of clay as we are.

Too muchness. Life demands more from us than we can deliver. Our parents always expected too much of us. People are forever asking us to do things we don't have time or talent to do. God asks too much. Whatever it is we are supposed to do, it is just too much.

Futility. Nothing that we do does any good anyway. Even if we had it in us to do some good, something out there is bound to prevent us from doing it. Something or somebody always snarls our intentions. So why should we hope to succeed when we know beforehand success cannot happen to us.

Going-nowhereness. One thing follows another as aimlessly as a string of link sausages. It is pretty much as Flannery O'Connor's hopeless preacher, Hazel Moses, saw it: "Where you come from is gone, where you thought you were going to never was there, and where you are is no good unless you can get away from it. Where is there a place for you to be? No place."[1] People who live by fate feel like empty cans on the assembly line at a soup factory, waiting to get only what fate will pour into them.

Some fatalists feel that they are fated by their own past mistakes: "I can never forget the terrible thing I did; I am stuck with it forever." Others feel they are fated by what other people did to them in the past: "I am doomed to fail because I was abandoned or abused or born black or brown or Frisian." The dyed-in-the-wool intellectual fatalist believes that we are *all* pawns of some blind cosmic force. Other people, who may not know the philosophical meaning of the word "fatalist," live by the hunch that the fight of life has been fixed.

The attitude typical of the person who lives by fate is *resignation*.

The attitude typical of the person who lives by faith is *hope*.

The person who lives by faith trusts that good things *can* happen because God wants good things to happen and is able to make them happen. Even when the odds are against their happening. When they don't happen, she keeps on waiting for them to happen. And even if something bad should happen first, she expects something good to come of it later on.

Faith, in one sense,[2] is simply a *readiness* for God. A kind of emptiness waiting to be filled, the way an empty cup held out by a beggar is ready to be filled. Or the way eaglets, with beaks open wider than the width of their bodies, wait for the mother eagle to fly back to the nest with food in her mouth. What God puts in the mouths of our faith is Himself.

Then, once *in* us, His spirit acts as the catalyst of hope that He will also do something *for* us.[3] And even when we feel a chill wind of failed hope shutting the door on what we had hoped for, we have a hunch that God will come back to open it to better things later.

I admit that I often have to hold on to faith by my fingernails. When people I dearly love are in trouble, I sometimes pray for them and then walk away with no real hope that God will actually do something for them. Maybe it is an age thing; maybe I have watched too many people get stuck in the groove of tragedy, with no relief from God that I could see. In any case, I still have to pray for faith *in* God before I get back my hope for others *or* myself.

Whether faith comes hard for me, however, does not cut much ice. I mention my struggle only to reassure other strugglers that they have company. I know for sure, by experience, that living by *fate* is hope's certain death. And I know that living by *faith* is hope's certain life.

∽

Just Remember This . . .

> We keep hope alive as long as we keep faith alive. Fate—
> the sense that everything that happens in life is settled in
> the game plan of necessity—kills hope. Faith—the open-
> ness of the heart to the possibilities of God—keeps hope
> alive.

Sum and Substance of Part Two

- Hopeful people keep their hope alive by taking responsibility for developing hope-building habits.
- Hopeful people
  - know what they hope for.
  - know which hopes are most important to them.
  - adjust their hopes to whatever new reality a failed hope leaves them with.
  - remember the times when good hopes came true and when good hopes crashed but they did not.
  - keep their eyes open for signs pointing to the possibility of what they hope for.
  - make regular reality checks on their hoping.
  - let other people hope for them when their own hope fails.
  - free themselves for a fresh future by forgiving people who spoiled their past.
  - live by faith instead of by fate.
  - believe that in a God-energized universe, life can be better than it is.

Part Three
When God Gets into Hope

Chapter 21

᭕

STANDING ON THE PROMISES

When God gets involved in our hoping, the odds get better, the stakes get higher, and the pain gets worse. The odds get better because God can do things for us that we cannot do for ourselves. The stakes get higher because if God fails to come through for us, we are not only disappointed that we did not get what we hoped for, we are left on our own, screaming at a deaf heaven. And the pain gets worse because it hurts more to feel let down by God than it does to be fleeced by dumb fortune.

Anyone who plants her hope in the soil of God discovers sooner or later that we don't always harvest all we hope for. Hoping *in* Him may improve the odds of getting what we hope for. But nothing except grace is a sure thing. So when it comes to what I have called our preferential hopes and our vital hopes, we are still—even with God in the game—in the hoping stage of life. Which means we still live by faith in possibility and not by guarantees of certainty.

God does make certain promises, however. And when we pin our hopes on His promise, we are getting close to the link between God and hope. God—as we all know—does not promise us everything we get it into our minds to hope for. But He does give us reason to believe that what He *does* promise is a commitment we can rely on. And God's commitment promises much more than possibility.

Which should not come as a surprise. Our most vital hopes in life are latched to the promises that ordinary people make to us. Our parents' promises. Our spouse's promises. Our friends' promises. We stake *everything* most precious to our lives on promises that have been made. And promises we expect to be kept. So when it comes to hoping for what God promises, we have already had plenty of experience with standing on promises.

When a person makes a promise to us, she comes as close as anyone ever can to giving us a snippet of certainty about the future. She sails out into our private sea of uncertainty and creates one small island of certainty in it for us. "Count on it," she says. "It is as good as done. I will be there for you, and I will see to it that it happens."

But *will* she? *Can* she? How can we know for sure? We can know for sure only in that intensely experiential way that we call trust. To be more specific, we have to trust her to have both the *intention* and the *competence* to keep her promise. Intention without competence is like a friend who invites you to dinner at an expensive restaurant and shows up with neither cash nor credit. Competence without intention is like a rich friend who invites you to dinner and never shows up at all.

So pinning our hopes on promises always boils down in the end to one thing: *trust in the person who makes them.* And everything depends on whether we know her well enough to justify our trust in her.

Back in the forties, Samuel Beckett wrote a play called *Waiting for Godot*,[1] which has become, critics say, a modern classic. What was the play about? Well, when the curtain rose, two men were standing on stage with their hands in their pockets, doing nothing, just staring at each other, men without a plan of action and without any gumption to act on it even if they did have a plan. All they did was wait—and hope—for Godot to come.

Who was Godot? They didn't have a clue. What would he do for them when he got there? They hadn't the foggiest. All they knew was that he had promised to come and that somehow things would be better when he got there. They trusted a stranger they did not know to come and do something for them, they had no notion what.

But Godot did not show. Ever. So the two men finally got tired of waiting and decided to leave. But they couldn't make a move. The play ends with them still hanging around with their hands in their pockets. Doing nothing. Just waiting. For who knows what?

A few years ago, on the anniversary of the play's opening, critics asked the playwright, "Mr. Beckett, now that fifty years have gone by, will you tell us who Godot is?"

"How should I know?" he replied.

It seems clear to me that Godot stands for the pipe dreams that a lot of people hang on to as an escape. From what? From their responsibility to make something of their own lives. Dreams that somehow, somebody—God knows who—or something—God knows what—will come and rescue them from their troubles—God knows how.

Believers know whom they are waiting for. He is the One who made the world and then, when His world went wrong, came down to earth to redeem the world He had made. He has a name: *Immanuel—the One Who Will Be There with You*. So when you have to wait for Him, you are not waiting for a nobody called Godot, you are waiting for a Somebody called God.

Once we know the difference between God and Godot, we also know what we are getting into when we pin our hopes on God: *whenever hope is based on a promise, hope and trust become one and the same thing*.

Look back to that strange moment in the far past when hope was born for all believers—back to Abraham and Sarah,[2] a couple nicely settled into retirement, looking for no adventures, wanting only some modest comfort in their own familial place. But sometime, in the dead of night perhaps, Abraham heard a voice, heard it with an inner ear that no sound waves ever touch, but heard it with a clarity that no one who heard it could question.

"Go," the voice said. "Go. Take Sarah and go."
"Go where?"
"Never mind, you will find out when you get there."
"But why?"
"Because I have chosen you to be the father of a new nation that will bless all the peoples of all the world."

Abraham, as far as we know, had never heard the voice before. The voice could have been no more than a rumble from his own soul. But Abraham knew that it was a real voice he heard, and he knew whose voice it was. How did he *know* that he knew?

I have sometimes wondered what Sarah was thinking when

she woke up before dawn and found her husband bustling about in the shadows with his foremen, loading down his pack animals and getting his flocks arranged for a long trek across the fertile crescent to the other side of his world.

"What in the world are you up to, my husband?"
"Packing, as you can see."
"Where are we going?"
"I do not know."
"But why are we going?"
"He told me to."
"Who's He?"
"God."
"How do you know it was God?"
"He spoke to me in a dream."
"Perhaps my husband only dreamed that God spoke to him."
"Good wife, when God talks to you, you *know* that it is God who is talking to you."

No one to whom God has surely spoken is open to rational alternatives. But Sarah would not have been the only one who wondered what had rattled Abraham's brain. His neighbors, in fact almost everyone in his whole world, especially the most pious, knew that there was nothing, there never had been, never could be anything really new under the sun. They knew for sure that whatever comes has been there before. And whatever goes comes back again. There was nothing new to hope for. Certainly nothing new to leave home and kin to find. Only heretics and fools thought there was. Unless, of course, a man of sound mind happened to have really heard the voice of God.

Abraham had heard. And there was no saying "no" to what God told him to do.

So that same morning Abraham led a compliant but worried Sarah by the hand and walked with her into the desert toward a place they could barely imagine and into a future they could not at all control. Thus began the odyssey of hope for the father and mother of all who put their hope in God.

What made Abraham go? For that matter, what makes people pin their dearest hopes on a promise from a God they cannot see or hear or touch? What could it possibly be but that confident, vulnerable, risky hunch we call trust?

This is the robust hope that neither persistent adversity nor massive tragedy can kill, the hope that lives after optimism drops dead, the hope that is nothing else but this: trusting the Maker of the Universe to keep His promises. It is the ultimate fall-back hope.

∽∞∾

Just Remember This . . .

> When God gets into our hoping, we pin our hopes on a Person. More exactly, on a Person and the promises He makes. Not that He will see to it that we get everything we wish for and believe is possible, but He will give us what He promises. So now our hope moves from a belief that the good we want is possible to a trust that God intends to keep His promise and is competent to do it.

Chapter 22

⁕

HOPING GOD WILL BE HERE WHEN WE NEED HIM

However, after Abraham's family had become, as God had promised, a considerable tribe, God disappeared and stayed offstage for four hundred years. A drought had dried up all the fertile fields of the land God had given to Abraham. So, at the invitation of the Pharaoh himself, the family had migrated into Egypt. But though they were permitted to prosper there for a while, an unfriendly Pharaoh came to power and made slaves of the lot of them. As we pick up the story, God's chosen people had been slaves in Egypt for four hundred years, and Abraham's great-grandchildren, whom God had promised to bless, felt cursed forever.

At last God decided that it was time for Him to get back to His chosen people. He showed up one day, totally unexpected and as a total stranger in a barren wilderness, to a shepherd named Moses. He appeared in a wisp of smoke coming from a dry bush that seemed unable to quit burning. Moses, who in better days had himself been a person of power in the land of Egypt but was now reduced to tending his father-in-law's flocks, happened to be nearby. He spotted the lingering flames and went to have a look.[1]

As Moses came closer, he heard a voice coming from the smoke, which was odd enough but not nearly as strange as what followed. For the voice was telling Moses to go back to Egypt and lead His people out of slavery into freedom. Lead them back to the same land that God had long before promised to Moses' ancestor, Abraham.

Moses balked. "I am no talker," he stammered. The voice brushed aside his tongue-tied modesty. "It does not matter what talents you have or what talents you lack, because I will be with you."

But Moses had another problem. A deeper one. It had to do with the identity of the Person behind the voice inside the smoke. Who was this invisible Stranger? Could He be trusted? How could Moses tell?

"Who *are* You? What is Your name?" Moses asked.

Any god's name in those days was supposed to reveal the sort of god he was. So the Stranger told Moses His name. The trouble is that we no longer know precisely what the name was. The best bet is that the name originally went something like this: "I am the One who will always be there with you—in My fashion."[2]

This was to be the fall-back promise for anyone who would ever find herself in a godforsaken place. As long as a person could trust God to be there with her, she would have reason to keep hoping. So even when she was denied her deepest, dearest hopes she could fall back on this one unspecified, but pivotal hope: that God would be on hand and that, with Him in the neighborhood, life could somehow, in some profound sense, get better than it was. But what is she supposed to do when she finds herself in a godforsaken mess that simply would not, could not have happened had God been there?

In Psalm 139,[3] the psalmist used three metaphors for places where we would never expect to find God—godforsaken places. The *places* stand for our *experiences* of helplessness and hopelessness. The psalmist was telling God that he expected Him to be in precisely those places where anyone with any common sense would know that God would not, could not be.

One metaphor is *the edge of the sea*: "If I take the wings of the morning and dwell in the uttermost parts of the sea, even there thy hand shall lead me, and thy right hand shall hold me."

The uttermost parts of the sea, the edge of the sea—as far as the ancient psalmist knew—was literally the rim of the earth. Beyond the edge, where the sea stopped, there was only a bottomless abyss, endless *nothing*. If you took one step too far, you would trip into a black hole of infinite nothingness where you would be beyond the reach of God.

Being at the edge of the sea is a metaphor for the experience of losing control of your life. When you sense that the foundations are shaking and that at any moment the bottom is going to drop out of your life, and you have no one who can reach down and pull you up, no one who can help you get your feet on the ground again; when not even God can stop your free fall into ruin; when, in short, you are a goner for sure, that is when you are at the edge of the sea.

But not to worry: if you should ever trip and fall out of God's presence, you will discover that He is there after all.

Another metaphor is *darkness*. "If I say, 'Let only darkness cover me and the light about me be night,' even the darkness is not dark to you, the night is bright as the day."

Darkness, in a manner of speaking, is the experience of being vulnerable, unprotected, and confused. You never know who is hiding in the shadows. You don't know which way to run. If you make a wrong move, you can fall and break your neck. To be in utter darkness is to be a sitting duck for trouble.

But not to worry: God will be with you when you are groping in your darkness. He can see in the dark.

The last metaphor is *sheol*. "If I make my bed in Sheol, thou art there!"

What in the world was *sheol*? Nobody can be precisely sure. It could have been the cosmic sewer littered with the stinking dead, rotted rats and decayed garbage and human bones. It could have been the dank underworld where departed spirits roamed and groaned. Or it could have been hell—the place of hot light and cold darkness, self-elected damnation.

Whatever the place was literally, it stands for our own private, inner, godforsaken experience. It stands for the awful times we know for sure that the jig is up with us, that we are alone, doomed, and damned—without God, without hope.

But not to worry: God will be there with you even when you have gotten yourself snared in hell.

This is what it means to hope *in* God. Hoping in God is hoping when there is no hope. Hoping in God is to trust that He will be there with us when we put our feet in places so godforsaken that He could not possibly be there even if He really wanted to be. He will be there holding us up when we are falling over the edge. Leading us through our private darkness. Being there—ahead of us, behind us, above us, under us, for us, and even *in* us—being with us when we land in places where things have gone to hell precisely because God is not there.

God does not take the forsakenness out of the godforsaken places. When people discovered God in Auschwitz, the death camp did not become a life camp. But when He comes to us in those places, He becomes our fall-back reason for believing that even though our situation is hopeless, we still have hope.

∞

Just Remember This . . .

> The most important thing we ever hope for from God is God Himself. Hope that He will be with us in our troubles. Not necessarily for Him to take our troubles away, but always to be there, under us to hold us up, ahead of us to lead the way, behind us to push us along, over us to keep an eye on us, and in us to keep alive our hopes of getting beyond our troubles.

Chapter 23

꩜

HOPING GOD WILL COME BACK

S imon Wiesenthal, then a young prisoner among the doomed at the Mauthausen concentration camp, was sound asleep one night when a young prisoner named Arthur, a dreamy skeptic of a fellow, grabbed his shoulder and shook him awake.

"Simon, do you hear?"

"Yes," he mumbled, "I hear."

"I hope you are listening [because] you really must hear what the old woman said."

"What could she have said?"

"She said . . . God was on leave. What do you think of that Simon? God is on leave."

"Let me sleep. Tell me when He gets back."

The next morning Simon wondered about the odd conversation he had had with Arthur and walked over to find him.

"What were we talking about last night?"

Arthur told him that Josek, a venerable prisoner whom Wiesenthal very much admired, had asked an old woman if she had heard any news. But she only looked up to heaven and prayed, "Oh, God Almighty, come back from Your leave and look at Thy earth again."

Which set Wiesenthal to thinking.

"One really begins to think that God is on leave. Otherwise the present state of things wouldn't be possible. God must be on leave. And He has no deputy."[1]

Yes, one really does begin to wonder. When I hear about all those hungry little kids running the streets of Rwanda with no father or mother to go home to because they have been shot, I cannot help wondering. When the one child born to us died, I wondered, *Oh, Lord, my God, You set me up. You promised to be with us, not once in a while, but always. But not today. Not now when I bury the little one I prayed ten years for. Why?*

At such times, my believing friends remind me of a line of a gospel song we all used to sing: "We will understand it better by and by." But I don't want to understand it better. I don't want to understand it at all. I don't want something that makes no sense to make sense. I would rather believe that God really has gone on leave of absence.

When God goes on leave, what do we do? What *can* we do? Hope He will come back—that is all we can do. We really begin to hope for Him precisely when things around us or inside us are going to hell before their time and our situation gets so filled with futility that we cannot think anything else but that God is not present and accounted for. "Hope comes alive," as that feisty, bad-news theologian Jacques Ellul insisted, "only in the dreary silence of God, in our loneliness before a closed heaven, in our abandonment."[2]

We may as well admit that it is mostly when our own private little world is falling apart—when it is *our* child who dies—

that we suspect that God has abandoned us. Deep pain tends to be a very self-centered experience. So does high hope. A whole tribe of people across the border could be dying from hunger, but while you are having an asthma attack you have energy to hope only for your very own next breath.

It was when *he* was going through his own royal hell that David, God's beloved King of Israel, knew for a fact that God had gone off and left him exposed, hanging by his heart from a weeping willow tree.

"My God, My God, *why* have You forsaken Me?"[3]

What can we make of such a question? Coming, as it does, from the same man who (in Psalm 139) knew for sure that God never, never abandons us, never *could*, that it just wasn't in God's character to go off and leave us.[4] What can we make of it when the Bible itself validates the most desperate of all questions?

The one thing we must by all means do is take David's question seriously. We must not suppose that he did not mean it. That all he really meant was: "It certainly feels *as if* You had abandoned me, even though I know You would not do such a thing to me." We get nowhere with his misery-smudged question unless we can believe that the man who asked it really meant it.

And it certainly is not as if David were asking *whether* God had abandoned him. He knew for sure that God had. The only question was: *why?* But David's why is not a thinking man's why. He was no musing intellectual; he was a bawling baby.

He was like a child who wakes in the night from a bad dream and wails in the dark for his mother. When our son Charley and his wife, Kimberly, a California native, were thinking about moving to Michigan they naturally talked about it a lot. One night they went out and left the two children with close friends. During the night, four-year-old Emily woke from a bad dream, called for her mother, and, when a stranger came instead, she wailed: "Mommy and Daddy have gone to Michigan." David in Judah knew for sure that God had gone to Michigan.

We also need to understand that such a cry is a wail of furious faith. Only a pit bull believer would say *my* God to the very God who had abandoned him. And only a person with total trust would have the chutzpah to demand an accounting from the Almighty. It is a rumble of faith, and this is why it is also a whisper of hope.

Finally, the question of why God has abandoned us get its answer only *when God actually does come back*. And it is not as if, when He arrives, God answers our questions about His troublesome behavior. His coming back *is* the answer. And it is the answer we really want. The child who cries for her mother gets the answer she wants the moment her mother opens the door, turns on the light, picks her up, and holds her tight.

Remembering his people's long wait for a sign that God might be coming back to South Africa, Archbishop Desmond Tutu admitted, "We might have been forgiven for wondering whether God was around, whether God saw, whether God heard, whether God was even aware of the suffering, the injustice, and the oppression. People detained, jailed, tortured. People exiled, people killed. All of this, it seemed, did not touch God."[5]

Why did God abandon them? Tutu heard the answer blowing in the winds when God finally did come back.

But does God ever *really* abandon us? Or do we only *feel* as if He does? I know that for devout people the very suggestion that God might ever leave us is unbearable, offensive. And yet the Bible often encourages us to wait patiently until God comes back; I have counted forty-three times that the prophets tell people that they will just have to wait for God.[6]

There is nothing we can do to force God to come back. We can only keep ourselves ready for Him when He comes. Meanwhile, we have to wait. "Wait on the LORD; / Be of good courage, / And He shall strengthen your heart; / Wait, I say, on the LORD!"[7] Job is the classic portrait of the person who waits and waits and waits and gets nothing for his waiting. "When I waited for light, then came darkness."[8] Isaiah, too, whose life's calling was to keep hope alive in the land, knew that waiting for the light could make the night interminable. "We look for light, but there is darkness!"[9]

So all we can do is make sure we are ready and waiting when He does come, hoping that the morning will come when we wake up to God and say: "Behold, this is our God; / We have waited for Him, and He will save us."[10]

Bad stuff, this waiting. Only hope gives us the stomach for it.

❧

Just Remember This . . .

> God seems to forget His promise to be with us and goes off on long leaves of absence. The inspired psalmist, for instance, was absolutely sure that God had abandoned him. But does He really abandon us? Or is He really always here, though in His own peculiar fashion? I cannot say. I only know that He sometimes gives us reason to believe that He has left us with nothing but hope that He will come back. Back where Immanuel belongs.

Chapter 24

❧

WHAT DO WE HOPE GOD WILL DO WHEN HE COMES BACK?

Suppose that as far as you can tell God has left you tread-
ing water, and you are too tired to swim. You keep hoping He will come back before you drown. You have
asked Him, begged Him, to come back. How many times?
But He is not paying attention.[1] Then one day you call Him
just as you had been calling Him every morning for five years,
and this time He answers: "Here I am. So what can I do for
you?"

Just suppose He asked that. What would you say? What I
am getting at is this: If we fret that God has gone, what is it
that we want Him to do when He returns?

I am not sure how I should put this. I do not want to tell
you what you should hope for. I cannot tell you what most
other people hope for. I only want you to wonder what it is
that you do actually hope for—something you wish for, something you imagine, something you believe is possible. So, to
give you something to compare your own hopes with, I shall

tell you what *I* hope for from God and why—when I wonder where He is—I keep hoping He will come back.

When God comes back, I hope that He will do some things just for me and mine. If He were to come back and ask me in so many words, "All right, I am at your service, what can I do for you?" I expect that I would first ask Him to do something about the acute needs of my favorite people. *Especially* my children and my grandchildren and my wife and my friends— heal their diseases, fix what is broken, keep them safe when the evil days come. This is what I pray for every day.

My request is cramped with selfishness, I know. But I'm not talking about what I *ought* to want from God. I am only talking about what I *do* want from Him. And I admit that, if the temperature of my daily prayers tells me anything about what I want most from God, my family is up there at the top of my list. But, once I move beyond my own intimate and tightly closed family/friend circle, I would, before I lost the ear of the Maker, get serious with Him about some of the persistently horrible things going on in the world.

When God comes back, I hope that He will do some of the really important things that need doing badly and do them as soon as possible. "For starters," I might say, "You could stop the killing; I don't know how You do these things, but I want You to get people to quit killing each other. I know that You want people to make their own choices and pay the price for making them, even when they make evil choices. But why should so many innocent children have to die just because of Your noble wish to honor bad people's free will?"

Once I dared to say that much, I would go for broke. Make life fair. Give poor people a break. Give crack babies a chance. Give people who live in the cross fire of violence a way out.

Bring people together. Make things work right for the ones for whom everything always goes wrong. I know that it is almost impossible to be perfectly fair to everybody. But does life have to be so awfully unfair?

When God comes back, I hope He will reassure me that He is still out there. When He stays out of my life for a while, I begin to doubt that He was ever really anywhere. And I want Him to come back just so that I can be sure He is out there— alive, personal, real, present, paying attention. But there is more. I want Him to become so personally real to me down here that I could not doubt Him any more than a lover can doubt that the person lying naked in her arms is real.

When God comes back, I hope He will renew my faith that my world makes sense. When I tell my left foot to move and it goes exactly where I tell it to go, nobody could convince me that such magical events could happen if God were not in it. But when I look at the wicked idiocy of people and the whimsical brutality of nature, I doubt that life has any rational plan or purpose behind it. So when I hope that God will come back, what I hope is that He will revive my faith that life has meaning. That beyond its barbarity and tragedies, beyond its sins and miseries, the story of our world has a beginning and a middle and eventually a very happy ending.

Hoping for God, then, is a way of hoping for meaning. And hoping for meaning is a way of hoping for God.

When God comes back, I hope He will give me hope. I hope God will come back to me and stoke the ashes of hope that almost died out when He was gone. Once, just once that I can remember, God actually came to me and said something to me to give me hope, said it so plain and simple that I "knew" it had to have been God. He came at a time when my family was being flogged by pain and I was lashing myself for not knowing how to make things better. I had been away for a few days when, driving up Sierra Madre Boulevard, I stopped for a red light only a mile from home; I was dreading to arrive and find out what had gone wrong while I was away.

That was when He came. He spoke just seven words, one sentence: *it is going to be all right.* That was all. If you tell me that what I heard was a wishful echo from my aching spirit, I could not prove you wrong. But I "knew" that it was God who told me that it would be all right, so I grabbed hold of hope the way a rock climber grabs a jutting ledge on a granite cliff.

Hoping for God is a way of hoping for hope. And hoping for hope is a way of hoping for God.

Sometimes I hope that God will come back and just be here. If I picked up the phone and heard God asking me what He could do for me, I might tell Him: " Nothing at all. I just want You back here." A lonely lover hopes her lover will come back to her, not to fix her leaking toilet, but just for him to be there with her, close. And when I am in touch with my soul's deepest desire, I want God that way.

Why does a lover want her beloved close to her? She will tell you: *he* is the reason. *He* is her joy. "Joy is the touch of God's finger. The object of our longing, [however] is not the touch but the toucher."[2] God is my joy sometimes, not always, but, oh, the joy of that sometimes joy.

᠆᠆᠆

Just Remember This . . .

> We hope for God to come back because there are some things we want Him to do or, maybe, just to be for us.

Everybody who hopes for God has his or her own reasons for hoping. So, since I could not tell you what it is that you want, or should want, I would simply tell you what I want:

- *I want Him (selfishly) to give my family and friends what they need and to do the same for me.*
- *I want Him to fix what is wrong with the whole world.*
- *I want Him to reassure me that He is real.*
- *I want Him to reassure me that my life and my world make sense.*
- *I want Him to give my hope a booster shot.*
- *I just want Him.*

Chapter 25

❧

SIGNS OF HIS COMING

When God comes back, how will we recognize Him? Mostly I recognize him *after* He has been here. In signs He leaves behind. Signatures. Footprints in the sand. Rainbows after a storm.

Ah, signs. Things that point us away from themselves to what we really want to see. Poets see them. Prophets see them. Children see them. Madmen see them. And so can we.

What turns an ordinary thing into a sign?

To say what I think about this, I have to tell a story.

The background to this story is a conspiracy of goodness carried on in a little French village under the long shadows of the Holocaust. The village was Le Chambon. About three thousand people lived there. Every last one of them put his or her life on the line day in and day out by hiding, all told, about six thousand Jews, mostly children, to prevent the French collaborators from carting them off to a concentration camp. Philip Hallie tells us about Le Chambon in his wonderful book *Lest Innocent Blood Be Shed*.

But the part I want to tell you about is something that happened to Hallie one day, after he had written the book.

He was talking about Le Chambon to a group of Jewish women in Minneapolis, and when he finished he invited his listeners to ask questions. A woman in the back of the room arose. There are, she explained in a French accent, many villages in France named Le Chambon. "Could you be speaking of the Le Chambon that lies in south-central France where the river Loire begins?"

Hallie replied, yes, his Le Chambon was that very village.

"Well, you have been speaking about the village that saved the lives of all three of my children."

Then she walked to the front of the room and asked if she might say one more thing. He recalls her wearing a sheath dress that made her body look like a slender cannon, taut, full of explosive power. But for a moment the cannon seemed to crumple.

"The Holocaust was storm, lightning, thunder, wind, rain, yes. And Le Chambon was the rainbow."

She and Hallie looked at each other.

"The rainbow," he said.

And she nodded.[1]

They understood each other. They both knew that the rainbow was the sign of hope after the great flood of the book of Genesis. *There* was a holocaust for you: corpses of all the people in the world, except Noah and his family, and almost all the animals of the world, too, bleached and bloated and rotting and stinking, piled from pole to pole in every crevice of every corner of the globe. Thick, black, creepy silence over the desolation of the earth. Surely God was not in that place.

But the rainbow came. And whenever it came for the rest

of time, it would remind God that He had promised never to destroy the world again. No more holocaust, not from God; from man, maybe, but not from God. The rainbow was a sign that God meant what He promised.

Almost anything can be a sign when it points us away from itself to something we want to find. Sometimes nobody else but us notices the signs we see. For me, some of the signs I see are my next of kin.

I called my oldest sister, Jessie, on a Saturday night a few weeks ago. For no special reason, just to chat. Jessie is eighty-five years old now, widowed, living by herself in Muskegon, Michigan, doing well. I asked how she was getting on.

"Oh, I feel terrific. I had such a wonderful day today."

"What happened today? What was wonderful about it?"

"Well, my friend Hilda, you remember her, the social worker? Anyway, she told me last week about a little girl, ten years old, I think, Amy is her name, who had been taken away from her parents because they were not good to her. Well, I woke up this morning and it was such a beautiful day, and I saw a notice about a play they were putting on for children at Oakview School and I thought maybe Amy would like to come with me to see it. So I called the home where she had been put and where Hilda works, and I told her I would like to take Amy out for a little while. Well, she said yes, so I took her to the play, and afterward we ate hot dogs and drank Cokes. Then we went to Lake Michigan, and we waded in the water and made some sand castles on the beach. Then we had some ice cream and went to see a training show that the army was putting on at the army base, and then I suddenly realized it was almost five o'clock, you know, and I just had such a good time that I hate to go to bed and end the day."

I saw God walking on the beach between Jessie and Amy. The sign pointed straight to Him, real as the shoes on my feet.

Sometimes one person sees a sign that God was there, while to another person the very same thing was a clear sign that God was far gone.

I was teaching a graduate seminar called *God and Psychotherapy,* and since we were talking about God, we eventually got to talking about prayer and whether therapists should ever pray with their clients if they asked for it. A few of the students said that their real problem with prayer was whether it did any good to pray at all, no matter what you pray for.

I admitted that I often had the same problem with prayer that they did, except that I had lived long enough to discover that God did come back sometimes to answer my prayers a while later, in His own time, and, of course, in His own odd fashion.

I told them about a time in my life when I was certain that God had deserted my adopted daughter Cathy. And me. At fifteen and sixteen, she was a rushing river of raging unhappiness. And I was a stagnant swamp of pain. All of her agony landed on one issue in her life: Who am I? And all of my agony landed on one issue of my life: Why can I not help her?

Let her speak for herself: "I was angry, rebellious, depressed and self-destructive. I did many things to hurt the people closest to me. . . . I had terrible arguments with my father in which I screamed horrible, angry curses at him. . . . I disregarded everything decent that my parents had taught me. . . . I did not comprehend my inner feelings [of] guilt, shame, and remorse for the things I was doing to hurt the ones I loved. But I know now that I was hurting them to see how far I could push them before they abandoned me too."[2]

In the dead of night I would sometimes fall facedown on the carpet and weep out Cathy's case with God. But God was gone. On leave of absence. Both of us felt abandoned. Betrayed.

But then He came back again, finally. Awfully late, I said, but He did come.

When I had finished saying these terribly personal things, a woman raised her hand and said she wanted to say something.

"I knew Cathy. I was with her in high school and went through it all with her. I watched you. I saw everything that was going on with you and Cathy and your family."

"I watched you through her eyes. And what I saw going on in your home was a sign to me that grace was real, and what I saw led me into a personal relationship with the Lord."

What was there for her to see? Misery, failure, doubt, resentment. Not a sign of God anywhere. Not that I could see. But she saw a sign. A sign of God. In our sad house. Mother Teresa saw God in the eyes of the poorest of the very poor whom everyone else supposed He had abandoned. Jesus expected us to see Him in the eyes of the naked, the prisoner, the hungry, the godforsaken. Maybe this young woman really did see a sign of God in my godforsaken house.

Later, Cathy herself *became* a sign of God. To me anyway.

Most of my signs are close to home. Doris's patience with me is a sign that God is with me. I watch my son's wife, Kimberly, in her intuitive wisdom, care for my grandchildren and see a sign that God is with them. I see my brother, Peter, in his eighties, spending a couple of days each week counseling troubled kids at a juvenile detention home. He's been doing it for years. He is another sign for me.

Oh, yes, I see signs of God in holy places too. At the altar when a minister puts his hand on my head and says a prayer for my healing. I look at a cross where people murdered the brightest and best of all the ages, and it is a sign that signals the very worst way of being godforsaken. And then I remember how God came back early in the morning a couple of days later to stir up life in Him again, and the empty grave becomes a sign that it will take more evil than we can do to keep God away for long.

And when I see signs, I also see hope.

❧

Just Remember This . . .

I've told you how I sometimes recognize God when He comes back after, as far as I can see, He has abandoned us. I don't recognize Him at first when He comes; but afterward, when I take a second look at what was going on I see His tracks. Traces of His having been here. I don't see Him doing miracles very often; I am more apt to catch Him in ordinary things, sometimes precisely in places that I had known for sure were godforsaken places.

Chapter 26

Who Wants to Go to Heaven?

ack in the days when I was teaching religion at Calvin College, I liked sometimes to tease my students with this pious, this sneaky question:

"How many of you want to go to heaven?"

Heaven won by a landslide. Always.

"How many of you would go there today if you had your choice?"

Most everyone preferred to defer the pleasure.

I would have waffled, too, had they asked me. I am not standing tiptoe on the tarmac eager to fly away to heaven before the sun sets. Maybe I would want to go there if I did not have to go by way of the graveyard. Maybe I would want to go there if I had more imagination. But, for the time being, I settle for a hope that when I do have to die (the later the better), my inner self will go on living, but in that other dimension, that better place.

Why would anyone be in a hurry to go to heaven? Among those who actually do want to go there, one might find a variety of reasons. Some seem to want to go to heaven because their experience tells them that this world is a rotten place. Or at least has become a very hard place for *them*. Others apparently want to go to heaven because this world is so splendid that it whets their appetite for something even better.

John Calvin, the master teacher of my particular religious tradition, felt both ways about it, depending on his mood. On one hand, nobody ever hated this world more than he did. He experienced it all as a "boundless abyss of all evils and miseries." And, to make a bad situation worse, he felt forced to live in this putrid cesspool trapped inside his "defective, corruptible, fleeting, wasting, rotting" body. With this miserable view of life, who would not want to go to heaven as soon as he could make a reservation?

But on a lovely June day in Geneva, Calvin had second thoughts. On such a day the earth did not look to him like a fetid swamp after all, but more like God's gorgeous garden home, with us His grateful gardeners. In such moods, he figured this way: God lets us "taste the sweetness of the [earth]" in order to whet our hope for heaven.[1] If what we have here can be this good, *how much better* the delights that await us.

Another of my teachers, Fyodor Dostoevsky, the profoundest of all storytellers, wanted both earth and heaven, not like Calvin with unrelieved ambivalence, but with straightforward passion for both of them at once. In *The Brothers Karamazov*—the greatest novel ever written—he put his passion for heaven and his love of earth in the mouth of a dying monk, the saintly Father Zossima.

"My life is ending," he said, "but every day that is left me I feel . . . in touch with a new infinite, unknown, but approaching life, the nearness of which sets my heart quivering with rapture, my mind glowing, and my heart weeping with joy."[2]

But the lure of heaven only reminded him of his love of this earth.

"Kiss the earth and love it," he pleaded, "love it with an unceasing, consuming love. Love all men, love everything . . . Water the earth with the tears of your joy and love those tears. Don't be ashamed of that ecstasy, prize it, for it is a gift of God, and a great one."[3]

If this life can be so good, *how much more* the life to come!

When my students told me they were in no hurry to get to heaven, I asked them one more question.

"Do you wish you would wake up tomorrow morning to discover that the person you loved most passionately loved you even more? Wake up hearing music you have always loved but had never heard with such infinite joy before? Rise to the new day as if you were just discovering the Pacific Ocean? Wake up without feeling guilty about anything at all? See to the very core of yourself and like everything you see? Wake up breathing God as if He were air? Loving to love Him? And loving everybody else in the bargain?"

All hands aloft. And I said, "I think you really do want to go to heaven tomorrow." My students, I think, knew the truth of what C. S. Lewis said about desiring heaven: "There have been times when I think we do not desire heaven, but more often I find myself wondering whether, in our heart of hearts, we have ever wanted anything else."[4]

When I do, which is rarely, itch for heaven I find that what I really want there is the fulfillment of all that is good about life now—but with its beauty never blotched with ugliness, its pleasure never choked by pain, its plenty never mocked by unfairness to others, its truth never hid by falsehood, its goodness never compromised by evil—and the discovery every day anew that our very beings are alive with God. In short, total fulfillment. Which is, I suppose, what we want when we want heaven.

The greatest theologian of this century, Karl Barth, notoriously wordy otherwise, used just one word to tell us what it is that we have when we have salvation: it is *fulfillment.* "Salvation is fulfillment, the supreme sufficient, definitive, and indestructible fulfillment of [our] being."[5] This, it seems to me, is what our hearts are most deeply restless for—our deepest desire, never totally experienced in this life—the total fulfillment of our very beings that is possible only in God. When we want this, heaven is what we want.

⚭

Just Remember This . . .

> Everybody wants to go to heaven, they say, but nobody wants to die. Well, none of the people I know are eager to die. They love this life too much to strain at the leash to get away from it. Maybe, however, in wanting the very best of this life, we are actually wanting to be in heaven. Heaven is never less than the good life we have here; it is all this and more. The good and beautiful that we see and feel here now and then is everyday stuff there. All this, and heaven too.

Chapter 27

❦

CAN YOU IMAGINE YOURSELF IN HEAVEN?

Very soon after we get something we have hoped for, we begin to hope for more. Hope never leaves us content with what we have so gladly gotten. It always ups the ante. And eventually our never-contented hearts hope for something that is not even available in the human potential catalogues.

Which is to say, we hope for a heaven—of one sort or other.

But we cannot really hope to be in heaven unless we can also imagine what we will be like if and when we get there. Not, mind you, what *it* will be like, but what *we* will be like.

You may recall that the two powers of our imagination— *outsight* and *insight*—stretch our vision in two directions: *outside* and *inside* of reality.

With *outsight* we can imagine almost any heaven we want and put it anywhere we wish. On a distant planet, perhaps, inside a universe not yet discovered, but to which we could fly on a spaceship if we had state-of-the-art instruments for navigation. Or maybe it is in a dimension where the very notions of space and place are obsolete. It could be no*where* and yet be more really "there" than any place on a cosmic map.

What we usually try to imagine with *outsight* are the living conditions of heaven. Will we chum around with old friends? Will we be able to contact the people we loved before we died? Will golden retrievers be there? Will there be a heavenly sex? With outsight we can imagine almost any heaven we want.

No matter, for the best thing about heaven is not what *it* will be. It is what *we* will be. Which brings us to *insight*. With *insight*, we don't imagine the sort of *place* heaven is, but the sort of *persons* we will be when we get there, wherever *there* is.

Not an easy thing this, imagining what we shall be like. It is not hard to recognize ourselves in what we once were. I look at a lanky, uncombed boy in a brittle, old snapshot, standing shyly, one foot on the board of a borrowed scooter, and I can recognize him as the very same person as the creaky codger I am now. But, if that sickly, skinny boy I once was could look at a snapshot of me at the crumbling age of seventy-seven, he would, I wager, never recognize me as the "him" he was one day to become.

In the same way, it may be easy for us, once in heaven, to recognize ourselves as the persons we were when we lived in our earthly bodies. But try to imagine yourself as a spirit without a body—a mind that thinks without a brain, sees without eyes, hears without ears, and touches without fingers; try this, and see if you can recognize that disembodied spirit as the very same person you are now.

When we try to imagine ourselves in heaven, we are best off, I think, if we ignore the *form* we shall take and stick to the *quality of persons* that we shall *be*.

We should see in our yearning for love the power to love someone totally with no effort at all. See in our fleeting moments of delicious happiness our potential for a delirious joy that never ends. In our nodding acquaintance with goodness see ourselves as good, clear through to the core of us. And ravishingly beautiful to boot. Then see our potential for intimate friendship with God in our restless longing to share ourselves with another person. This is insight into ourselves, enough insight to recognize in ourselves the potential to be the persons we want to be and will be in heaven.

Maybe the easiest way to recognize the invisible spirits we shall be as the very selves we are, is to imagine ourselves having the qualities that we admire so much in our good friends. This is the advantage of having close friends who are the sorts of persons we wish we were. It is also the advantage of having a portrait of Jesus in the New Testament, a well-focused, if incomplete, portrait of the sort of person He was and the sorts of persons that we will be, each of us in his or her own fashion, a good deal like Him.[1]

Some of our truest images of ourselves in heaven, though, are stirred up by bread-and-butter pleasures we enjoy here. Have a thigh-thumping laugh at a ridiculous story, and you get a sharp snap of yourself happy in heaven. Let a piece of soul music send shivers down your spine, and you have an image of your capacity for beauty in heaven. Watch a giggling two-year-old toddle into his mother's arms, and you get a fairly good image of yourself in heaven with God. Maybe the happiest memories of ourselves on earth are our clearest images of what we shall be in heaven.

Just Remember This . . .

> *It may not be all that hard to imagine what life in heaven is like. Remember that the best part of getting to heaven is becoming the sorts of persons we were always meant to be, and in our better moments wanted to be, in the loving company of God and all of His children. Once we think of it this way, we can relax while we wait to see with our own eyes what we can only imagine here.*

Chapter 28

⟨⟨⟩⟩

CAN WE EVER BE SURE?

O n some sad afternoon that we had hoped could be postponed, they will lower our corpse into a deep hole dug specifically for us, and a minister will confront our loved ones with the assurance that they are putting our body in the cold ground "in the sure and certain hope"[1] of our resurrection to eternal life. Odd thing to say about hope, "sure and certain." Hope is what we do precisely when we are *not* sure; "hope so" equals "maybe so." This being the case, a "sure and certain hope" begins to look like an honest to goodness oxymoron, something like painless toothaches and cubed basketballs.

If our hope is "sure and certain," we must be talking about a very special kind of certainty. And a special *reason* for being that sure.

As far as I can tell, we have no hard evidence that we shall live after we die. On the other hand, we have no hard evidence that we will rot along with our rotting bodies. So, if we need convincing material evidence before we can be sure of heaven, nobody—it seems to me—can be sure, one way or the other.

Every argument *against* our carrying on as spirits after we die assumes that no such thing as spirits exist. It goes without saying that *if* we are only biological computers, neurological engines, bits and blocks of DNA but no more, there is no "we" to keep living when the machine breaks down.

People who are "sure and certain" that there is no such thing as a human spirit sometimes feel compelled to explain why sane and intelligent people persist in believing that our spirits live after our bodies die. Sigmund Freud had a predictable explanation: we *believe* that we will survive dying because we *wish* we *could* live forever. Like children who refuse to grow up, we insist that what we want to be so really is so.[2]

Freud's explanation of our childish belief in eternal life is roughly like saying that if I see myself lolling at a sandy beach on the Canary Islands, my wish to be there is what makes me believe that there really is such a place as the Canary Islands. But could it not be just the other way around? Could it not be that I wish to lie on the beach on the Canary Islands precisely because the Canary Islands and its beaches are there for me to lie on?

In the same way, could it not be that so many people wish for heaven precisely because there is a heaven to be wished for? Do we not long for a deep and lasting love because love is real? Do we not wish for a good friend because friendship is real? May we not want to know what life is about precisely because life is about something? And may we not wish for eternal life because it is our destiny to live forever?

Let's put the shoe on the other foot. Say that Freud knows that we all die like dogs because he really—in his subconscious—wishes to die like a dog. But anyone who knows that he will die like a dog cannot die like a dog because anyone who knows ahead of time that he will die like a dog is not a dog.

> A dog
> that dies
> and that knows
> that it dies
> like a dog
> and that can say
> that it knows
> that it dies
> like a dog
> is a man.[3]

Freud was "sure and certain" that he would die like a dog. Is it not just as reasonable for me to be "sure and certain" that I shall die like a god?

But even if believing that we live after we die is as reasonable as believing that we die like dogs, the question remains: What makes us so *certain* about it?

As far as I can tell, we can be sure of heaven only if we are sure of God. We are sure of God only if we have learned to trust Him. Trust is the only way to be sure when we do not have objective reasons for being sure.

I will risk a comparison. I am "sure and certain" that Doris, who has been my wife for fifty years, will stick with me to the end, no matter what happens. What makes me so sure? I am sure because I have experienced her as a person with loyalty bred in her character the way running is bred in the bones of a thoroughbred. So when I hope she will stay with me, I am hoping with the "sure and certain" hope that she will. Such hope is otherwise known as *trust*.

In fact sometimes we are so sure about the eternal life we hope for that to deny it would be like denying that the stone you just stubbed your toe on is a real stone. When the love of his life, Joy Davison, died, C. S. Lewis wrote: "Anybody who knew her knows that if she is not alive, then she has never lived." It has to be so; love will not have it otherwise. And thus it is not only *possible* that it is true, and not only *certain* that it is true, it is *impossible for it not to be true.*

What this all comes down to is that our "sure and certain" hope of eternal life is a special, personal, and unprovable kind of certainty that we call trust. We know it will happen because we trust someone to make it happen. We stand on the promises.

⌒∞⌒

Just Remember This . . .

> Some people do not want a "hope so" religion; what they want is a "know so" religion. But when it comes to heaven, what we have is a "hope so" sort of "know so." A "sure and certain" hope. Sound like gobbledygook? Not if you consider how one gets to be "sure and certain." This "knowing so" comes by way of trust. Simple trust in God, the same way I know that my wife loves me and will never leave me.

Chapter 29

❦

Is There a Happy Ending?

Hoping for God eventually brings us to the question
that haunts every person who loves God's good earth
and is daily dismayed by the sin and folly that bleed
it: What will come of it all? All of our efforts to create a decent
world for human beings to live in together? All of the great
civilizations? All of the villages and the universities, the vegetable gardens and the cathedrals, the parks and the poetry—
what will come of them all? When we push our sights beyond
our closed circles of intimate hope for ourselves out into the
whole human story, what is there to hope for?

It seems to me that all the hopes people have for the long-
term future of the world winnow down to four choices.

The Hope of Endless Progress

This was the hope of the enlightened optimists of a century or two ago. They took stock of our rich human potential,
and what they saw convinced them that our minds were wise
enough, our hearts good enough, our intentions firm enough,

and nature friendly enough to guarantee that nothing could sidetrack the train of human progress.

It was not as if optimists believed that we would ever reach utopian perfection. What they foresaw was more like an irresistible advance toward a more perfect imperfection. No matter how good things got, they would keep getting even better. We could count on it.

As we all know, the high hope of endless progress fell wounded in the trenches of the First World War and then perished in the fires of the Holocaust. Endless human progress ended in endless human wickedness.[1]

The Hope of Mucking Through

This is the chastened hope of the disenchanted idealist. He has lost faith both in human powers to make the world work right and in God's intention to come back and make it work right for us. He is a realist and for him, any hope for a perfect society—or even a steady progress toward it—is a utopian pipe dream.

The realist's best hope is that the human family can keep hobbling along pretty much as it has until now. Not even this shrunken hope is a sure thing, not by a long shot, but if we can keep ourselves from poisoning the earth or destroying ourselves, we have a reasonable chance of keeping the great global show on the road. The world may get even better for the lucky and the plucky, but it is likely to get even worse for those with neither luck nor pluck. There is no hope at all that the whole world will ever work right for everybody.

Still, if we can't make the world work right, we can keep binding the wounds, stanching the flow of blood, cooling the hottest spots of violence, and improving our life-prolonging technology. With a bit of luck and a dose of human decency, we may keep mucking our way through the disasters that the evil spirits of the world will always be threatening us with. All things considered, we have enough going for us to justify our hopes of creating a moderately livable future for at least the fortunate minority of tomorrow's children.

The Hope of Surviving the Burning of the World

This is the hope of the faithful who take the dire, apocalyptic prophecies of the Bible as literal descriptions of what is going to happen to the world. They have no hope at all for the world. They are certain of its annihilation. They do not hope that God will save the world. They hope that God will demolish the world after they are raptured into heaven.

It is the hope that I grew up on. My mother worried a lot about the end of the world. She saw signs of its end in every disaster's headline. A freighter going down in Lake Michigan or an earthquake in Arabia were signs to her that the end was at hand. Then there was the anti-christ; he showed up everywhere—in the guise of Mussolini, of Hitler, maybe even Franklin Roosevelt; maybe we would have to wear the mark of the beast—666 on our foreheads to get so much as a handout from the New Deal. But that would be only the beginning of trouble.

We learned at church that, before the end comes, the whole world will pass through a time of terrible tribulation. Mountains will slide into the ocean, earthquakes will happen in diverse places, and blood will run to the shins in the Battle of Armageddon. About this time Christ will appear in the sky, and those who are prepared for Him will, in the twinkling of an eye, be snatched from whatever has their attention at the moment and will rise from the earth to meet Him in the air. Then God will put the torch to the world.[2]

It was never something that I could get myself to hope for. God's beautiful creation turned into a cosmic cinder? All too terribly sad. Sad for us. A lot sadder for the Creator.

The Hope of Global Remodeling

This is the hope of those of us who love this world, grieve for its sins and sorrows, and have a stubborn faith that God can fix it. Rebuild it. Make it new—all of it. But especially the human part: our lives together, our lives with Him.

We do not want the world to end. We hope for what the Bible calls *Shalom*, a grand word packed with every good thing that any human heart could want or need: Peace. Prosperity. Love. And joy, abounding joy. All fairly distributed; a world remodeled. Like a 1930s kitchen remodeled, ceiling to baseboard—brand-new, yet the same kitchen, only now a bright and handy culinary control center. A world made new, a world that will make God and all His children happy again, yet the very same world He created, with its plains, its valleys, its mountains, its rivers, its oceans, and, yes, even its cities.

That wise British curmudgeon Malcolm Muggeridge, as his mental powers got less and less reliable, was able now and then—with a clarity I could covet in my very best days—focus with sparkling joy on just two "extraordinarily sharp impressions" he had of his life and his world:

> The first [impression] is of the incredible beauty of our earth—
> its colours and shapes, its smells and its features; of the enchant-
> ment of human love and companionship, and of the blessed
> fulfillment provided by human work and human procreation.

And the second, a certainty surpassing all words and thoughts, that as an infinitesimal particle of God's creation, I am a participant in his purposes, which are loving and not malign, creative and not destructive, orderly and not chaotic, universal and not particular. And in that certainty, a great peace and a great joy.[3]

Yes, yes, yes, this is exactly how I feel. What I hope for is the remaking of God's immensly lovely world. And in this hope I, too, find a "great peace and a great joy."

⌒∞⌒

Just Remember This . . .

Of the four available scenarios for the way things will ultimately turn out for our groaning, hoping planet, I set my hope on the new earth, the kingdom of God on this very earth I stand on. A very happy ending for a very sad world. Much happier than slogging its way interminably between tragedy and triumph. Much happier than burning to a cinder in a global holocaust. It is the hope that this world, the one we live in and love so much now, this world, God's world, will end up far better than ever, and better than ever forever.

Chapter 30

❧

MY VERY WORLDLY HOPE

Acouple of years ago, I drove my Toyota alone from Los Angeles to Grand Rapids, Michigan, a trip of about fifteen hundred miles. As I pulled onto the 210 freeway a few blocks from my house, I reached, as I almost always do at such a moment, for the FM radio button. But on a contrary impulse I pulled my arm away and decided to drive for a while without the chatter and the music. By noon, getting on toward Las Vegas, I had decided to do without the news, and the talk shows, and my Mozart tapes for the rest of the day.

The next morning it dawned on me that I had liked driving the freeway without distracting sounds to clutter up my interior conversation. So I decided to do without radio and tapes all the way to Michigan. Maybe in five days of highway solitude a new insight or two into the strange ways of God with His world might slither into my mind.

I did it. I bought gas by sliding my Visa card through a slot in machines that did not tell me to have a good day, and I said only what I needed to say to get a motel clerk to give me the

169

key to a room I could sleep in. I prayed some to God and talked to myself a lot.

What mostly came to me, however, were not deep thoughts, but gospel songs that we sang at the Berean Church in Muskegon, Michigan, to which my mother shuffled the five of us children two miles each way twice every Sunday and where, no matter how it had begun, the sermon ended with either the Battle of Armageddon or the Rapture of the saints. So I broke my silence by croaking such verses as I could still recall, surprised at how much the old hymns of coming glory still affected me. One of my favorites was "Beulah Land."

> Oh Beulah Land, sweet Beulah Land,
> As on the highest mount I stand.
> I look away across the sea
> Where mansions are prepared for me,
> And view the shining glory shore,
> My heaven, my home, forever more.

I surely did like to sing hymns about that shining glory shore back at the Berean Church. But now I was singing about it while driving through the pure, purple canyons of Utah, with their pinstriped shadows drawn by a softly dying sun along the screen of parallel crevices in the eastern canyon walls, and I knew for sure that I did not now and never had ever really wanted to live in Beulah Land. Not as a forever guest. This world of Utah canyons and the society of human beings with bodies is where I want to live, linked one day with all of God's children in a society where justice and peace embrace.

I know that the apostle Paul said that he would rather go to heaven that moment than to stay here on earth another day.[1] Some philosophers and mystics have also longed[2] to be transported from this material world into a spiritual Beulah Land. For them, even the best of all possible worlds can be no more than a shadowland. What they hope for is to lay aside their fleshly baggage and live as pure spirits in a realm of light without shadows, gazing at and drinking in God's beauty and truth and goodness in the full joy which only a disrobed spirit can feel.

There is, however, another biblical version of what there is to hope for. It is the vision, not of our ascent to heaven, but of God's descent to earth. It is the hope that He will come back to fill the world with Himself and make the whole world good again, from sea to shining sea. A place where all of His children will finally feel at home together. And at home with Him.[3]

The way I read the Bible, heaven—the place of departed spirits—is a sublime intermezzo. A rest stop where our spirits learn to enjoy God while we wait in bodiless patience for God to shape His earth into His peaceable kingdom. So, when it comes to my *forever life,* it is in this world, repaired and renewed, my Father's world, my native place, where I hope to live it.

Or do I? Really? The way I hope my pension will weather the storms of Wall Street? The way I hope that my children and their children will be well? Am I chafing at the bit for God to come and make the world work right? How can I tell whether my hope is genuine and not just talk, the kind of talk religious folk are expected to talk?

Do you remember the three ingredients of all hope? They can be a simple way to test whether we really do hope for what we say we hope for. Or what we think we *ought* to say we hope for. It is a test with just three questions:

Do I really—with all my heart—wish for a world that works right?

Can I imagine what life would be like if the world did work right?

Do I believe it can happen?

If you answered yes to all three questions, you probably are an active member of the new world hope club.

DO I REALLY WISH IT?

I heard a preacher say once that if your guts are not twisted into knots and your heart isn't broken into small pieces because of the pain other good people suffer and the evil that bad people do, you cannot be sincere when you say you hope that God will one day make His whole world work right. When I think about the thousands upon thousands of crack babies and aborted babies and starving babies and abused babies and abandoned babies in the city of Los Angeles, I do wish, wish with all my being, that God would fix His world. But at other times, when the troubles of my own people and my own life get too much for me I spend so many of my most passionate wishes on my own small circle that I have little energy to wish good for strangers. I own up to it. And it makes me wonder how genuine my pious hopes for the poor and oppressed people of the world really are.

Just to test the sincerity of my hope that God will come and fix His world, I imagine myself having this conversation with Him:

Me: O God, I beg You to come back and make the world work right.

God: Playing praying again, Smedes?

Me: No, it is no game this time, Lord; I really do want You
     to come and stop the killing and give Your peace to the
     world.

God: All right then, I will come. On one condition.

Me: What's the condition?

God: That you give up your own salvation.

Me: You mean that You will come if I am willing to burn
     in hell? Or can I just die, stay dead, oblivious of my
     own rotting?

God: Yes, I am willing and, yes, in your case, extinction will
     do.

Me: Do I have to die today?

God: I'll give you a couple of months to get ready.

Me: Lord, You've got a deal.

I don't really believe that God would ever negotiate such a
deal with anyone. But what *would* I say if He really were to give
me a chance to die for the world? I believe that I would be willing to give up my place in God's renovated world if that were
the only way to persuade God to come back and fix it. But I cannot be sure. Anyway, dying for the world is not the hard part.

The hard part comes when He tells me to show my passion
for a world that works right by living the sort of life that makes
people say: "Ah, so that is how people are going to live when righteousness takes over the world."[4] This, not dying, is the hard part.

"Show Me!" He might say. "Show Me what you are *doing*
now to make your own neighborhood work right. Show Me
what you are doing to bring a little more justice into your
particular cranny. Show Me what you are doing to turn a place
where people hate each other into a place of love, what you

are personally doing to restore some peace where people are at each other's throats. Show Me! I will not believe that you really do wish for the whole world to break out in Shalom one day[5] until I see you sacrificing a little more to bring a bit of Shalom into your neighborhood.

After hearing God's "show Me" I wonder if my wish that God would come and fix His world is after all a pious cover for my shame at having done so little for the wretched of this world. Maybe the only people who really want a new world are the ones who have been victims of much evil in this world. Maybe only the people who have left their pleasant places to go and live with the poor and downtrodden can sincerely wish for the kingdom of God.

Still, I really do wish for a world where every last child is loved and every poor person has a life at least as good as mine and everyone who is a stranger to God becomes His friend. Even if my wishing is half-baked, I do wish that God would come and convince all the world that His way of love and justice is the best way. And as long as I am at least half sincere about it, my wishing brings me to the threshold of a genuine hope.

So much for the wishing. I thought it would be the easy part. But the easy part may be the imagining, which I thought would be the hardest part. Can I imagine this whole wide wicked world becoming good again in all its parts and in all its ways? For every last child of God? I think so. But let's see.

CAN I IMAGINE IT?

Almost anyone, it seems to me, can imagine waking up in a world where nobody ever points a gun at another of God's creatures, where children dance in the city streets at night and never need to be afraid, where no man ever abuses a child and no child ever abuses a woman, where no mother ever has to watch her child starve, where no child is ever born unwanted and where all the poor people of the whole world have more than enough of what they need.

Anyone who has been smashed by man's inhumanity can imagine a world where life is at least fairer and kinder than it is now. Anybody who has been hurt by other people's meanness can imagine a world where we would all treat each other with respect. Any child is able to imagine a world where grownups are always gentle and kind, and where God can always be seen in the face of any neighbor. Where all of us, of every color and every culture and every race, will join hands, reconciled together and reconciled with God, and sing hymns at heaven's gate to the glory of the world's Redeemer.

This much, surely, anyone with a mole's vision can imagine.

Even the book of Revelation, with all its puzzling symbols, is as plainspoken as a Vermont farmer on this: *God is coming to earth to stay with His people forever* and when He comes "[He] will wipe every tear from their eyes; there shall be no more death, nor sorrow, nor crying; and there shall be no more pain, for the former things have passed away."[6]

And once the bud of *imagination* begins to blossom into hope, our hope will itself, as Jurgen Moltmann said it would, "provide inexhaustible resources for the creative, inventive imagination of love."[7]

Do I Believe It Is Possible?

If the world *will* be fixed depends on whether it *can* be fixed. Is our world a fixer-upper? If the world—by which I mean human society in its countless modalities—is beyond repair, we may as well forget the whole thing.

Are there any signs that the world still contains a sound foundation for God to build on? I think so. Sometimes signs of goodness show up right in those places where the wounds seem beyond healing.

On the night before Yom Kippur, in 1997, an eight-year-old Israeli boy named Yuval Kavah was run over and killed by a car on a busy street in Tel Aviv. On the same night and in the same hospital where they had brought Yuval, a little Palestinian girl named Rim Aljaroushiu was dying of a failing heart. Yuval's grieving parents offered their son's still-beating heart to any child who needed it. Rim was chosen. After the surgery was done, the Israeli mother and the Palestinian mother embraced each other, sharing tears of joy and grief, as a Jewish boy's heart beat inside a Palestinian girl's breast.

When a mother of Israel gives the heart of her son to a child of Israel's enemy, I see a sign that this world has not broken down beyond repair, a sign that it can be salvaged and made to work right again. And maybe, if we have the imagination to see them, we can find signs on any main street.

A four-way stop sign respected day in and day out could be a sign. A house rebuilt by Habitat for Humanity is a sign. A converted political crook who did his time and is now serving the inmates of our prisons with the soul-renewing grace of God—a sign. A family of working poor people holding out together against gang invasion of their neighborhood—a sign.

The fact that the world *can* be fixed does not guarantee that it *will* be fixed. I grant you that. We also need a reason to believe that God is ready and able to make His world work the way He intended it to work when He made it.

I cannot find human wisdom and human goodness pure and powerful enough to support my hope. Nor am I convinced that a righteous world is the awaited end point of human evolution. I certainly do not consider nature to be so benign that it will make up for our moral deficiencies; in fact, I do not think nature cares a fig about what happens to us in the end.[8]

I will show my hand here and say that the only reason I can find for believing that the whole world might ever work right is God. If He really created the world, and if He really was so committed to it that He gave His only Son, not to condemn the world but to save it,[9] it is—as I see it—not merely possible that He intends to fix it but unthinkable that He would *not* intend to fix it.

But do we have any *reason to believe* that even if God does really *intend* to do it He *has what it takes* to fix the world?

Early Christians wondered about it. Christ had come, had died and come back to life, but He went away again, and nothing had really changed. Their friends and neighbors told them to open their eyes and see that nothing basic ever changes, never has, never will. And so they pressed the apostle Peter: Is it true what they say? Is the world never going to change for the better? What are we waiting for? The apostle answered this way: "In keeping with [God's] promise, we are looking forward to a new heaven and a new earth the home of righteousness!"[10]

Waiting for a new earth! Ah, yes, the long wait, hope forever deferred. The interminable wait has seduced masses to follow their Hitlers, their Maos and their Lenins as they took it into their calamity-prone hands to force the world into the mold of their own madness. It has led others to settle more safely for an endless slog through the swampy mush of good and evil that the world has become. Some of us, however, keep waiting for God to come and make everything work right. Why do we wait?

Because He promised. Ah, yes, the promise again. It is the believer's reason and her only reason to keep waiting for a new and better world. Still, a promise is only as good as the intentions and competence of the one who makes it. Is there any reason to believe that God has good *intention* of fixing the world? And any reason to believe that He has the *competence* to do it?

We do know this much for sure, if He does not intend or if He is not able to fix His own world, nobody else is going to do the job for Him. So if He is not bent on seeing it done or is not up to doing it for us, hope is a cruel illusion.

There is one sign in particular that, after all the years since it was set on a hill outside a city wall, still signals God's good *intentions* to keep His promise. It is the cross to which they nailed Jesus of Nazareth.

The Cross still signals to Christian believers that the Maker of the Universe chose to die, in a manner as incomprehensible as it was horrible, in order to save the world from its own self-destruction. He must at least have good intentions of keeping His promise to fix the world.[11]

But good intentions are one thing. Competence is another. Do we have reason for believing that He is up to the challenge?

After two millennia, there is one sign that keeps telling us that God has what it takes to make good on His promise. Has what it takes to overcome the worst of the world's disasters. It is that baffling but wondrous thing that happened one early morning as the fingers of the day's early light were filtering through the flora of a burial garden in Jerusalem. The thing that happened when the life-birthing energy of the universe's Maker began to pulse inside the dead biological remains of the very Jesus whom God had apparently abandoned two days before. The cells regenerated themselves and He, body and soul, came back to life.

Any rational skeptic will remind me that ancient rumors of a rabbi's resurrection make a thin limb on which to hang the hopes of the world. Yes, I would admit, it is a thin limb. But sturdy enough, for all that, to have held up a sign for all these ages that God the Creator has the competence to renew the world He made.

Nobody has hoisted the sign of hope in a more hopeless time than has Desmond Tutu, Archbishop of South Africa. Here he is—during a total blackout of optimism, without one credible piece of evidence to show that things were ever going to change—here he is, I say, exploding with hope that a new world was coming:

> The resurrection of Jesus is our guarantee that right has tri-
> umphed and will triumph over wrong, that good has tri-
> umphed and will triumph over evil . . . that love has triumphed
> and will triumph over hate. You and I know . . . despite all
> the evidence to the contrary that we, black and white together,
> are one in the Lord, and we will hold hands, black and white
> together, with our heads held high as we stride into the glo-
> rious future which God holds out to us.[12]

Tutu closed his ears to the street-smart realists who told him that a "glorious future" for South Africa was a pipe dream. And so I too will close my ears to the realists who tell me that the good world I hope for is nothing but a warmed-over version of a Utopia that never has been, never will be, and never can be. As long as there is an Easter, we will have one good reason to keep on hoping—while we also keep on groaning and keep on fearing and keep on doubting—that God will come back and make the whole world good for all of His children.[13]

Life is going to win! Peace is going to win! Love is going to win! Justice is going to win! God is going to win! Creation's story is going to have a happy ending.

> This is my Father's world,
> And let us ne'er forget,
> That though the wrong seems oft so strong
> God is the ruler yet.

∞

Just Remember This . . .

Our ultimate hope is not to escape a damned world, but that God's will shall be done in His redeemed world. We truly hope for the renewal of the earth only if we really wish for it. We actually hope for it only if we can imagine it. And we will hope for the renewal of our world only if we have reason to believe that God can and will make it happen. My own reason for believing that it will happen is God Himself, the God who "makes all things new." Believers are not optimists, they are people of hope. Their only reason for so huge a hope is the story of how the Maker of the world once came to His world, died, lived again, and still intends to come back and fix His world once and for all.

Sum and Substance of Part Three

- When God gets involved in our hoping, hope becomes trust in a Person and the promises He makes.
- God promises three main things:

  He promises to be with us even when life tells us that He has abandoned us.
  - When life feels as if God has left us and forgotten us, hope is the energy to wait for Him to come back.
  - When God seems to abandon us, hope gives us reason to ask what we want from Him when He comes back.
  - Hope develops eyes for signs of His coming and often sees them quite close to home.

  He promises that His children will live after they die.
  - We hope for heaven only when we *wish* to go there. One way to know whether you wish to go to heaven is to wish for the best God can offer us here and now.
  - We hope for heaven only if we can *imagine* ourselves there. One way to imagine ourselves in heaven is to

imagine ourselves as the persons we are meant to be.

- Hope for heaven is a "sure and certain" hope in the sense of implicit trust in God's promise of heaven.

He promises to make our world work right again.

- God promised that He will not desert His world and that His creation has a fine future.
- His promise gives us reason to believe that the ultimate destiny of the children of God is not the disembodied life of heaven, but an embodied life on God's good earth.
- In short, God's story and the story of our world will have a happy ending.
- The reason for believing that God can give the world a happy ending is that God is committed to His creation and gave us a sign of His ability to remake it when He raised Jesus from the grave.

The sum and substance, then, of what happens when God gets into hope is this: God becomes our fall-back hope and when He does, He is the One who keeps our hope alive.

ONE MORE STORY BEFORE WE GO:
THE HILL OF HOPE AT SIAULIAI

I f you had ever visited Lithuania before the Russians came
and had taken the Siauliai-Ryga road for nine miles east of
the village of Siauliai, you might have come on the Hill of
Crosses. It is a mound of earth about thirty feet high, covered
with homemade crosses that villagers had planted upright in
the ground. A forest of crosses it was then. High iron crosses,
towering like lodge pole pines over an underbrush of stubby,
wooden and cement crosses. You could hardly see the ground
for the crosses.

Each cross represented a loved one who had died as a
stranger in exile or in prison, a Russian prison most likely. The
Hill of Crosses had been sacred to the villagers for a hundred
years. It was a mystic place to them, a holy place where the
pious gathered almost every day to pray and remember.

Then, in 1940, the Russians came. To the Soviet army the
crosses were nothing more than a superstitious insult to rational atheism. So they made a law against cross planting.

But it did them no good. Villagers sneaked in under the cover of night and planted their crosses anyway. The Russians rolled in their bulldozers. They burned the wooden crosses, buried the cement crosses, melted the iron crosses. But still the people came, one or two at a time, and planted their crosses at night. And still they came to pray during the day.

At last, in 1988, the Russians gave up and left the Hill of Crosses in peace.

Now the crosses have taken on a new meaning for the people of Siauliai. People cluster around the hill now and remember how the mighty Russians mustered their machines against their crosses and how the crosses beat them back. Each cross planted during the time of occupation when it was forbidden to plant them has become a reminder that more things are possible than they had dared dream of then. The hill of memory has been transformed to the hill of hope.

Hope is a strange invention -
A patent of the Heart -
In unremitting action
Yet never wearing out -

Of this electric Adjunct
Not anything is known
But its unique momentum
Embellish all we own
                              —Emily Dickinson

NOTES

Chapter 1

1. Taken from *Bullfinch's Mythology*, Modern Library. (New York: Random House, n.d.), 15 ff.

2. Karl Menninger, "Hope," in Simon Doniger, ed., *The Nature of Man* (New York: Harper and Row, 1962), 186.

3. In one of his inspired eagle flights over the human condition, St. Paul observed in Romans 8:20–21 that the story of all creation is a tale of groaning and hoping, and that none of those who believe in God are exempt from either the groans or the hopes.

4. I learned to put it this way from the Jewish philosopher Hannah Arendt's important book called *The Human Condition* (Chicago: Univ. of Chicago Press, 1958).

5. The French philosopher Gabriel Marcel wrote a book about hope to which he gave the title *Homo Viator*, which is Latin for "Traveling Man." His point was that creatures who have traveling in their blood need hope because they can never be sure of getting where they are going. Marcel, *Homo Viator: Introduction to a Metaphysics of Hope* (Glouster: Peter Smith, 1978).

6. What psychologist Erich Fromm once said must be true: "If man has given up all hope, he has entered the gates of hell—whether he knows it or not—and he has left behind him his own humanity." Erich Fromm, *The*

Revolution of Hope (New York: Harper and Row, 1968), 58.

Chapter 2

1. C. S. Lewis, *Letters of C. S. Lewis*, ed. W. H. Lewis (New York: Harcourt and Brace, 1966), 289.
2. In Philippians 4:11, St. Paul said that he had learned to be content in whatever state he was. I am sure he meant exactly what I mean by "contented discontentment," and that this contentment is possible only by keeping hope alive.

Chapter 3

1. James T. Patterson, *Grand Expectations: The United States, 1945–1974* (New York: Oxford Univ. Press, 1996), 483.
2. Mary Warnock, *Imagination* (Berkeley: Univ. of California Press, 1976), 9.

Chapter 4

1. Hebrews 11:1. This profound but obvious truth is the insight that Robert Schuller, in our time, has translated into "possibility thinking" and made the prevailing message of the most successful religious television program of all time.
2. Marcel, *Homo Viator*, 51.
3. Jacques Ellul, *Hope in Times of Abandonment* (New York: Seabury, 1973), 229.
4. John Macquarrie, *In Search of Humanity* (New York: Crossroads, 1983), 243.
5. Alex Bein, *Theodore Herzl* (Philadelphia: The Jewish

Publication Society of America, 1941). See also Paul Johnson, *A History of the Jews* (New York: Harper and Row, 1987), 395 ff.

Chapter 5

1. Eugene O'Neill, *The Iceman Cometh* (New York: Vintage Books, 1957).
2. In "The Commandment to Hope: A Response to the Contemporary Jewish Experience" in *The Future of Hope*, ed. Walter H. Capps (Philadelphia: Fortress, 1971), 69.
3. Norman Cousins, *Head First: The Biology of Hope* (New York: Dutton, 1989).

Chapter 6

1. Ginker and Spiegel, *Men Under Stress* (Philadelphia: Blakiston, 1945), 131 ff.
2. Ellul, *Hope*, 205.

Chapter 7

1. Fromm, *Revolution*, 8.
2. Nelson Mandela, *The Long Walk to Freedom* (New York: Little, Brown, 1994), 431.
3. "The decision to wait is one of the great human acts." W. Lynch, *Images of Hope* (Notre Dame: Univ. of Notre Dame Press, 1974), 177.
4. T. S. Eliot, "Four Quartets," in *T. S. Eliot: The Complete Poems and Plays* (New York: Harcourt Brace, 1952), 126–127, italics mine.
5. Josef Pieper, the noted German philosopher, "Hope is the power to wait patiently for a 'not yet' that is the

more immeasurably distant from us the more closely we approach it." Peiper, *The Virtue of Hope* (New York: New American Library, 1963), 40.

Chapter 8

1. The conversation is from Wallace Stegner's beautiful novel, *Crossing to Safety* (New York: Penguin, 1971), 289 ff.
2. William Lynch wisely warns: "Nothing leads to more hopelessness than the naïve theory that everything can indeed be hoped for." Lynch, *Images,* 61.
3. Ibid., 48.

Chapter 10

1. The scene is described a bit differently in the book from which the film was made. Here, Thomas Keneally describes the German officer as saying to himself: "If you hosed the cars for people, you were making them promises about a future. And would not such promises constitute, in anyone's code, a true cruelty?" Thomas Keneally, *Schindler's List* (New York: Wheeler Publishing, 1994), 357.
2. Fromm, *Revolution*, 20.
3. Romans 8:23.
4. Christopher Lasch, *The True and Only Heaven* (New York: W. W. Norton, 1991), 530.
5. To pursue the possibilities of this "other" hope, any reader may leap over to Part III.

Chapter 15

1. Yechiel Eckstein, *How Firm a Foundation* (Brewer, Mass.: Paraclete Press, 1997), 130.

Chapter 16

1. Gary Wills, "What Makes a Good Leader," *Atlantic Monthly*, April 1994, 63.

Chapter 18

1. Max DePree, *Leading Without Power* (San Francisco: Jossey Bass, 1997), 125.

Chapter 19

1. Any reader who may wish to investigate the ways forgiveness affects hope may wish to consult three books on the subject that I have written: *Forgive and Forget* (Harper/San Francisco, 1984), *Shame and Grace* (Harper/San Francisco, 1993), and *The Art of Forgiving* (New York: Ballantine, 1996).

Chapter 20

1. Hazel Moses is the preacher on the run from Jesus in Flannery O'Connor's *Wise Blood*.
2. In another and critical sense, faith is a decision to believe that certain things about God and Christ are true.
3. Romans 15:13.

Chapter 21

1. Samuel Beckett, *Waiting for Godot* (New York: Grove Press, 1954).
2. Genesis 12:1–6.

Chapter 22

1. The story is found in Exodus 3.
2. The name has four consonants but no vowels. Ancient

Hebrew, as written, had no vowels. Moreover, as it turned out, the Hebrews considered the name with the four consonants too holy for human lips, so it never acquired vowels in spoken Hebrew. For this reason, translators could only guess what the name was. The translation I am using is taken from the great Catholic scholar, John Courtney Murray. J. C. Murray, *The Problem of God* (Cambridge: Yale Univ. Press, 1967), 9–ff.

3. Psalm 139:8–12.

Chapter 23

1. Simon Wiesenthal, *The Sunflower* (New York: Shocken Books, 1976), 13 ff.
2. Ellul, *Hope*, 177.
3. Psalm 22:1, italics added.
4. Psalm 139:1–13.
5. Desmond Tutu, *The Rainbow People of God* (New York: Doubleday, 1994), 195.
6. One might ask whether God leaves us because we have made such a mess of things on His good earth. Or has the world gotten in such a bad way because God went off and left it? Probably both. One thing is sure: God did not turn the shop over to us because we had gotten smart enough and good enough to manage it on our own. It could be worse. Instead of leaving us on our own for a while, He might have wiped us out, the way He did in Noah's day. So we at least have time to hope.
7. Psalm 27:14.
8. Job 30:26.

9. Isaiah 59:9.
10. Isaiah 25:9.

Chapter 24

1. The prophet Jeremiah promised the abandoned exiles that God would come back to them and that when God came back He would be there for anyone who really wanted Him: "You will seek Me and find Me, when you search for Me with all your heart" (Jer. 29:13). But Job sought Him with all his heart and did not find Him. "Oh, that I knew where I might find Him" (Job 23:3). Job finally found Him all right, but only after God returned from His leave of absence.
2. Peter Kreeft, *Heaven, the Heart's Deepest Longing* (San Francisco: Ignatius, 1989), 156.

Chapter 25

1. Philip Hallie, *Lest Innocent Blood Be Shed* (New York: Harper/Collins, 1985), xvi–xvii.
2. Catherine Smedes, "Damaging Words, Secret Information, and Severed Ties," manuscript, 1996.

Chapter 26

1. John Calvin, *Institutes of the Christian Religion*, J. T. McNeill ed., transl. by F. L. Battles (Philadelphia: Westminster Press, 1960) III/9/1–5.
2. Fyodor Dostoevsky, *The Brothers Karamazov* (New York: Random House, 1950), 348.
3. Ibid., 387.
4. C. S. Lewis, *The Problem of Pain* (New York: MacMillan, 1962), 143.

5. Karl Barth, *Church Dogmatics*, IV/1 (Edinburgh: T & T Clarke, 1956), 8.

Chapter 27

1. 1 John 3:2: "Now we are children of God; and it has not yet been revealed what we shall be, but we know that . . . we shall be like Him."

Chapter 28

1. The traditional funeral phrase—"sure and certain hope"—is distilled from Hebrews 6:18–19.
2. Sigmund Freud, *The Future of an Illusion* (New York: Doubleday Anchor, 1957).
3. I found this poem by Erich Fried in Hans Kung, *Eternal Life* (New York: Crossroads, 1991), 162.

Chapter 29

1. There are many scholarly studies of the optimism of the Enlightenment. A recent study that may be the most readable of them all is Christopher Lasch's superb book, *The True and Only Heaven: Progress and Its Critics* (New York: Norton, 1991).
2. Besides the hundreds of books and tracts that promote this and similar versions of the world's end, I have found a very objective survey of the many versions of apocalyptic hope in Paul Boyer's splendid book, *When Time Shall Be No More: Prophecy Belief in American Culture* (Cambridge: Harvard Univ. Press, 1992).
3. Richard Ingrams, *Muggeridge: The Biography* (Harper/San Francisco, 1995), 241.

Chapter 30

1. "For I am hard pressed between the two, having a desire to depart and be with Christ, which is far better. Nevertheless to remain in the flesh is more needful for you" (Phil. 1:23–24).

2. Philosopher Peter Kreeft wrote a wistfully beautiful book about hope for an unworldly heaven with this revealing title: *Heaven: The Heart's Deepest Longing.* My own title would more likely have been *This World Remade: My Heart's Deepest Longing.*

3. Isaiah and the other prophets of the Old Testament never hoped that the Messiah would lead us out of this world; they hoped for him to come *to* this world and make it work right. Jesus Himself quoted the words in which Isaiah wrapped the hope of all the prophets: "He will not crush those who are weak or quench the smallest hope until he brings full justice with his final victory. And his name will be the hope of all the world" (Isa. 42:1–4; Matt. 12:18–21).

4. This is, in fact, exactly what Jesus tells us to do in what we call the Sermon on the Mount.

5. At the very end of what is no doubt the most profound book about hope to appear in this century, Jurgen Moltmann writes: "The world is not yet finished. . . . It is therefore the world of possibilities, the world in which we can serve the future, promised truth and righteousness and peace." Jurgen Moltmann, *Theology of Hope* (New York: Harper and Row, 1967), 338.

6. Revelation 21:3–4.

7. Moltmann, *Theology,* 34.

8. A man said to the universe:
    Sir, I exist.
    Nevertheless, replied the universe,
    That fact has not created in me
    The slightest feeling of obligation.
    Joseph Katz, ed., *The Poems of Stephen Crane: A Critical Edition*, by Stephen Crane (New Jersey: Cooper Square, 1966), 102.
9. John 3:17.
10. 2 Peter 3:13.
11. This was the apostle Paul's logic: If God did *this* much for us we have reason to believe that He must intend to do the rest (Rom. 8:32).
12. Tutu, *Rainbow People,* 40.
13. Romans 8:21–22.

ABOUT THE AUTHOR

Lewis Smedes has been married to his wife, Doris, for fifty years and lives with her in Sierra Madre, California. They have three children and two grandchildren. He taught Ethics at Fuller Theological Seminary until he retired in 1994 at the age of seventy-four. He is the author of *Forgive and Forget, Shame and Grace, Mere Morality, The Art of Forgiving, A Pretty Good Person, Choices,* and *Caring and Commitment.*